ADVANCE PRAISE

"With her vast experience of working with families of all kinds—foster, adopted, biological—Erin shows us how kindness can transform even the most challenging situations. Read this book for its downright practicality in how it addresses the nitty gritty of everyday life with your children."

— **Shefali Tsabary, PhD,** Author of *The Conscious Parent* and *Out of Control*

"Connection and Kindness are two themes that Erin embraces in her writing, as well as the way in which she lives. In her first book, Erin artistically and generously blends her experiences of parenting with her professional perspective as a therapist and parent coach, working with foster and adoptive families. She inspires and invites us to take that courageous step into self-aware, conscious parenting, to grow in the understanding of its importance so that we can truly be connected with our children. Readers of this book will be gifted with Erin's gentle, yet powerful insights on how to authentically honor yourself, your children, and your relationships with them."

—**Georgia P. DeClark, MA,** PCI Certified Parent Coach®, Preschool Director and Teacher Founder of Georgia DeClark Parent Coaching, LLC

"Erin Taylor has written a book that every parent on the planet should read. There are no parenting tips or tricks in this book. Erin beautifully recognizes how stories touch our hearts and have the power to transform our parenting. Erin's deep wisdom from years of working with children, parents, and foster parents shines through her personal and professional anecdotes that speak to the soft heart inside each of us, the part of us that yearns for true connection throughout our children's lives and that knows what to do. Erin Taylor has written a treasure trove of wisdom that no "how to" parenting guide can compare to. She inspires us to be amazing parents by opening us to truly seeing our children's souls, by slowing ourselves down enough to appreciate the sweet moments with our children, and by caring for ourselves abundantly so that our fulfillment naturally spills over to our families. All this book requires is that you dive in and absorb the stories with a whole heart. When you do, your parenting transformation will happen quite naturally."

—**Sheila Wenger,** Lead Instructor at The Parent Coaching Institute, PCI Certified Parent Coach ® at The Parent Partner, LLC

"With original insights that are derived from personal experience on parent-child attachments and how to restore them, this is a book for revitalizing families & preserving self—a must read for every parent."

—**Karen Ognibene, MA,** Editor South Jersey MOM Magazine

"This book will touch the deepest strings of your heart and invite you into a new level of connection with your child and to life itself. Erin has the gift to transform daily events we all experience as parents into profound opportunities to nurture our children's souls in a loving, intentional and practical way. Her writing is engaging, honest, and takes us by the hand on a gentle trip into our hearts. *Connection and Kindness: The Key to Changing the World Through Parenting* is a reflection of the beautiful human being and highly experienced professional Erin is."

—**Patricia Barros, MD (Brazil),** PCI Certified Parent Coach®

"Connection and Kindness: The Key To Changing The World Through Parenting shares stories, wisdom, and good vibes that remind us to make connection and awareness our most important parenting tools. Erin generously shares her personal and professional experiences and inspires each of us to tap into our own compassion and authenticity. This leads to self love, deeper relationships within the family, and eventually, societal change."

—**Cathy Cassani Adams,** Author of *Living What You Want Your Kids to Learn* and host of Zen Parenting Radio

"In Erin Taylor's book, *Connection and Kindness: The Key to Changing the World Through Parenting*, parents and caregivers are reminded about the power of kindness. As a teacher, coach, and single mother (Sophie, age 4) I work with children all day long. When working with other people's children I spend a great deal of time trying to meet their individual needs. Before reading Erin's book I'd come home to my daughter and often my patience seemed to have vanished. I found myself easily frustrated by the littlest things. After reading Erin's book I've been able to reflect on my parenting practices. As a result, I find myself consciously focusing on how I address my daughter. Recently, we were having a battle over something minute. I walked away from her angry and frustrated. Erin's book entered into my mind. I went to her and said 'Mommy isn't being very kind right now, is she?' I picked up Sophie and hugged her. We talked through the situation. Erin's book reiterated what I already knew: my daughter deserves the level of patience and understanding that I tend to reserve for others. From now on, I will let kindness be my guide when it comes to parenting Sophie."

—**Janet Liimatta**, STEM Teacher, Grades K-5

"This book is about much more than kindness. It articulates the simple yet profound wisdom of living in relationship with our children. Erin's wisdom is packaged in stories of children and parents that could be from any of our life experiences, told with an honesty and vulnerability that makes the wisdom easy to access as we relate it to our own children and our own parenting."

—**Gloria DeGaetano**, Founder, Parent Coaching Institute

"Kindness: a well known, and one would think, simple word. Who would imagine that this word would be the foundational principle of a book on parenting, yet the concept of kindness is highly applicable and powerful in the experience of parenting. In this day and age of a myriad of books on the subject of parenting, how can one hope to find any real guidance in a parenting book with kindness as its foundational message? I am pleased to report that there are many pearls of wisdom for parents found in Erin Taylor's book, *Connection and Kindness: The Key to Changing the World Through Parenting*.

In reality, kindness is not so simple a word. Erin does a wonderful job defining and describing the many ways that kindness is personified in effective parenting by helping the reader understand the more complex concepts that underlie it.

The beauty of Erin's style is that she explains these concepts in a casual, conversational way that makes the reader feel as if she is gaining profound support from a visit with a dear friend. Some of the pearls of wisdom that Erin passes on to her readers revolve around subjects such as:

• The difference between seeking compliance and seeking connection with our children and the profound connection that happens when we as parents detach a bit. (Paradoxical, I know. But you will understand when you read the book.)
• How a shift in perspective helps parents to respond very differently when dealing with misbehavior. With a newfound perspective that all children want to do well, the

parent learns to respond to misbehavior from a place of compassion instead of fear. From this new place of compassion, the response to misbehavior is to seek connection and show support instead of reacting quickly and doling out discipline.

• The beautiful experience of building connection that endures beyond the boundaries of life itself.

• Why striving to fulfill yourself as an individual is not only important for your well-being but is vital to being the best parent you can possibly be to your children.

• Why negotiating with your teen is much more productive than compromising with them, not only to bring more peace to the parent-teen relationship, but also for instilling tools in our teens that help them have healthier personal and professional relationships in their adult years.

• The deleterious effects of parenting with fear and how important it is as a parent to help a child conquer their own fears. (I especially loved Erin's description of fear as a mirage that evaporates when confronted!)

• Various principles for busy parents to tape up on your mirror and read every morning while brushing your teeth. (My suggestion, not hers... but they are that good.)

• Love as seen through the eyes of kindness. Erin shares her unique reflections on parental love at its best.

While Erin's book beautifully supports any parent in the throes of raising children, she also presents many personal experiences from her work as a counselor of foster families that provide the foster parent reader with the awareness that she really understands their unique experience of parenting as well. If you are looking for a wonderful read that balances presentation of applicable information with the comforting support of a great friend, I highly recommend this book.

As an experienced family counselor, parent coach and mother, Erin has much wisdom to share. I highly encourage you grab a cup of tea and settle in with her after the kids are tucked into bed."

—**Lisa Kenawell,** PCI Certified Parent Coach®

"Connection and Kindness: The Key to Changing The World Through Parenting is a treat for everyone. This book touches one's heart from the first page. It is written in such a way as to grab our attention, make us feel alive, emotional and deeply entrenched in the stories. I found my heartstrings pulled in different directions by both the teachable moments Erin so brilliantly shares as well as the heartfelt difference she and her family make in the community. Anyone who purchases this book will be graced with the opportunity to feel the blessings that Erin shares, the extreme power of her writing and the incredible teachable moments, lessons and moving stories that comprise this amazing book.

I guarantee you will not be disappointed. Instead you will be elated, moved and inspired by this authentic and wonderful book. Its inspiring words and stories will make you want to share Erin's wisdom!"

—**Sue DeCaro,** PCI Certified Parent Coach®

"In the hustle and bustle of non-stop parent pickups and drop offs and our societal views of the perfect family/parent one thing seems to be lacking in our children and ourselves. That is kindness. Erin states 'from the time our children are born, they are moving toward adulthood every step of the way.' The questions you ask as the caregiver or parent are: What has your child grown into? What path are they taking? Do they have kindness? Not just towards siblings but towards themselves?

Life goes by in an instant and, if we are not careful, our children become adults in a blink of an eye. *Connection and Kindness: The Key To Changing The World Through Parenting* is like having a cup of tea or your favorite latte with Erin. She writes about her passion, her family, the hopes to have others connect with their children, and the kindness to get them there. The relatable stories of her own children from school to sports to her own on-the-job training make the book come alive with meaning. From the moment you are on their cruise with Selvin, *Connection and Kindness* takes you on a self-reflective journey towards your own meaningful connections with your children, spouse, neighbor, friend, or complete stranger.

This journey toward kindness is not perfect. Mistakes are made and triumphs are celebrated but the desire and drive to connect with one another is a bond that once established in truth is forever."

—**Kimberly D. Mueller, EdD, NBCT,** First Grade Teacher, FL Walther Elementary School

"Erin Taylor's book about kindness makes it all seem so simple–and it is–yet why does something so simple require us to work so hard? As a parent and counselor who is too often living a hurried life, Erin's book reminds me about how important it is to take a step back, smell the flowers, be appreciative for what is in front of me and be present in the moment. As parents, it is important to take time for ourselves to rejuvenate and explore what is going on with us too. It is our job to be attuned to our kids and look beyond their behaviors to what those behaviors are trying to communicate to us. Letting go of traditional punitive parenting (which is sometimes based too much on control and too little on trying to actually understand what is going on with our kids) is important. It is truly amazing how far a simple conversation can take you with your kids as a parent if you take the time to have it and don't just look for that quick fix, which often results in negative interactions and exchanges between parent and child. Erin's book shows us that being kind to others as well as ourselves can make a profound impact on not only our children's lives, but also others and our own. It is through teaching our kids these skills that we can bring hope and compassion to others and teach our kids to be well-rounded and less-stressed adults."

—**Terri Havers, MA,** Mental Health Professional Working with At-Risk Youth & Treatment Home Families

Connection
& Kindness
The Key to Changing the World
Through Parenting

ERIN TAYLOR

IT TAKES A VILLAGE
PUBLISHING

Connection & Kindness
The Key to Changing the World Through Parenting
Erin Taylor

FIRST EDITION

ISBN: 978-1-942545-15-6
Library of Congress Control Number: 2015946499

Artwork by Tina Paparone.

Published in the United States of America

It Takes A Village Publishing,
An Imprint of Wyatt-MacKenzie

IT TAKES A VILLAGE
PUBLISHING

www.villageparentcoaching.com

*To **Jay** – my best friend and love of my life.*

*To **Sydney** – my angel in Heaven, and to **Noah**, **Faith** and
Brady – my beloved children on earth –
you are the apples of my eye and my greatest teachers.*

*There are no words to accurately describe the deep
gratitude and love I have for all of you.*

CONTENTS

FOREWORD

by Dr Shefali Tsabary

All around the world, in homes of many different kinds and in many different societies, parents are becoming aware that the old disciplinary way of raising children, where the parent is the sole authority and dictates to the child, simply doesn't work well in our more democratic era.

Children are subject to so many more influences today than that of the primary family, so that in nation after nation they increasingly grow up in societies that prize freedom. Now, if we try to raise our children in the old ways, when they reach their teens they simply rebel, and we lose all control along with all possibility of influencing them for the good.

In the global shift that's underway, parents are learning to listen to their children's needs and work cooperatively with them, setting appropriate boundaries where needed, but principally negotiating rather than laying down the law. Connecting with a child, so that both parent and child understand each other, is today the defining element in parenting. When we connect instead of constantly correcting, our children don't resent us. Because they sense that we honor them for the unique individuals they are, they are more willing to listen to us.

I call this approach to raising children "conscious parenting." Instead of dictating, reacting without thinking, and taking the approach of "because I said so," when we parent consciously, we think about what we are saying and doing instead of just cutting loose. We *use* our head instead of *losing* it.

When we truly begin listening to our children, seeking to understand who they are instead of imposing our will on them, it brings up our own unresolved issues from childhood. We have to face up to our own impatience, tendency to control, untidiness, tardiness, anger, or whatever other ways in which we too lack self-control.

Allowing our children to be a mirror to us of our own emotional immaturity, our refusal at times to listen to them, and our other unconscious behaviors becomes a means of growing ourselves up alongside our children. Raising a child then takes the shape of a partnership that's fruitful for all concerned, the result of which is that our children grow up to be self-disciplined, self-determined, cooperative human beings who are ready to go out into the world and live a fulfilling and productive life.

At the heart of this revolutionary way of parenting is an essential quality, without which all the insight we may have into how to raise a child simply won't work. That quality is *kindness*.

In this beautifully written book, Erin, who is a specialist in counseling and coaching foster, adoptive and biological families, takes us into the lives of her clients as they struggle with extremely difficult circumstances and behaviors. She also invites us into her own home, where we see how she and her husband are learning from their children how to be kind in everything they say or do.

By showing us how kindness makes all the difference in all sorts of everyday challenges, Erin has given us a book that can help us all to become the loving parents we know at heart we have always wanted to be.

– Shefali Tsabary, PhD
Clinical psychologist, author of the
Oprah acclaimed and
New York Times bestsellers
The Conscious Parent and
Out of Control

INTRODUCTION

by Erin Taylor

I have known since I was 11 years old that I wanted to help families—kids and parents—to have better relationships with each other. Growing up, I always liked school, but I could never articulate what my favorite subject was. I enjoyed my teachers and classmates and I enjoyed the schoolwork, but it really did not excite me. However, I did not realize how unexciting it was until I got to 11th grade and took my first Psychology class. I tried to enroll as a 9th grader but was told I was too young. It was so hard to wait those two years, as I was very excited to dive into something that I just knew I would love. So 11th grade Psychology class was where what I had always known about myself became solidified: *I want to help people improve their lives and in the process, change the world.*

Fast forward to college application time. I would be the first person in my family on either side to go to college, and that fact alone was very intimidating. I always knew that I was capable of succeeding in college, but I was still a bit scared. What if the work was too hard? What if I was not cut out for college? And unfortunately, I had no one I could turn to for reassurance that these were (what I would learn later on) completely normal fears to have in high school. When it came to majoring in Psychology, I got serious cold-feet, wondering if I was really "smart" enough to succeed. Since I was on the yearbook committee my senior year and enjoyed laying out the pages, I decided that I would major in graphic arts, but I made sure that the college of my choice also had a Psychology program.

I want to mention the college of my choice for a moment. I have always been a person who has naturally allowed intuition to guide me, long before I even knew what I was doing. When the time came to apply to college, I applied to several, but met a co-worker at my part-time job over the holidays who went to Drexel University. As soon as she said the name, I knew that was the place I was meant to go, even though at that time I had never heard of it and knew nothing about it. But I immediately set about gathering information about the school and found it was just perfect—a city setting, about two hours from home (not too close and not too far), and having both a graphic arts program and a psychology program—perfect!

As soon as I knew it met all of my requirements, I knew deep in my heart that I was meant to go there. There was even something about the name of the school that sounded so "right" and so very familiar—as if it had been a part of my life forever. People would ask me what I would do if I did not get accepted into Drexel. Whenever they said that, my insides would want to shout that there was no possible way that could happen—that I would not get into Drexel. And I did not feel this from a place of denial—I felt it in my soul; I knew deep in my soul that this was where I was meant to go.

Fast forward to Christmas of my senior year. My dad had an accident at work—a head injury that left him in a coma two days after Christmas. While he was in the hospital fighting for his life, my mom and I kept a vigil at his bedside for four straight weeks until he came fully out of his coma and spent the next three months in a rehabilitation hospital for head-injury patients. While he was laying there in the coma in the ICU, I got my acceptance letter for Drexel. I was so excited to tell my dad and I wanted desperately for him to be able to celebrate with me, but I took comfort in the fact that even though he was still on a respirator at that point and was not able to open his eyes or talk, he was able to wiggle his finger when we asked him a question. So when I told him my good news, he wiggled his finger like crazy. My heart was bursting with joy and gratitude on so many levels at that point.

So, having chickened out on the major part, I entered Drexel as a graphic arts major. That lasted only two quarters as I struggled my way through introductory art classes and my projects got torn apart in critiques by my professors—I could feel the life draining out of me. Nearing the holidays, I walked to the train station to purchase a ticket to go home. While I was at the station, I became mesmerized by this family who was also purchasing tickets. The boy looked to be about nine years old and he had longish, black, greasy hair. The mom was clearly under the influence of something and could not even walk straight. As the mom said goodbye to the dad who was dropping them off at the station, the little boy became the parent in the situation, for when the bell rang announcing their train's arrival, the boy took his inebriated mother's hand and said "Ok mom, when we go down these steps, I want you to hold my hand and not get lost."

Have you ever had one of those moments in life where the world seems to come to a grinding halt as time stretches out before you in slow motion? This was one of those times. I felt like I was being pulled into their struggle as if being sucked in by a black hole. I watched them, transfixed until they descended the steps out of my sight. Then I turned on my heel, went straight back to my advisor's office, and promptly changed my major to Psychology. I graduated Cum Laude from Drexel in 3.5 years and then went on to get my Master's in Counseling Psychology from Loyola University Maryland.

One other note about Drexel before I continue. Looking back, the two reasons that I was destined (and knew as much in my heart) to enroll there was because of this scene that I witnessed at the train station that would properly set the course for my career, and because I met my future husband there in the spring of our freshman year. Meeting him was another one of those moments where the earth seemed to stop spinning and time stood still as I felt my world aligning as it should. We have been together since then and happily married for 18 years so far.

I have worked for the past 18 years as a counselor with foster and biological families and have loved it. But several years ago, I worked with one family who I was not able to get through to and who was causing me serious burnout. This left me in a bit of a crisis, wondering if I needed to abandon my life's work and begin a different career. A series of events (which I cover later in the book) shifted my life's course to become a PCI Certified Parent Coach ® which has been deeply fulfilling for me.

Reverse a few years: When my husband and I got married, we immediately set about trying to build our family with no success. Three years and thousands of dollars in fertility treatments later, our precious daughter Sydney was born. But she was born with a very serious heart defect and tragically died at the age of 24 days old. Another one of those time-standing-still moments as I got sucked in by a black hole, only this time it was horrific and gut-wrenchingly painful. But I knew in an instant that I wanted to keep a journal of my first year of grief in the hopes that one day I would turn it into a book to help other bereaved parents survive the death of their child. I faithfully kept that book all through the years—through more fertility treatments and the births of our other three heart-healthy children and my growing up as a parent. As time and circumstance guided me down my life's path, I found myself in a conversation with an editor-friend of mine talking about this book that I had wanted to write for years. By the end of that conversation, he had me convinced that the time did not seem right for that type of book and instead, I should write a book about parenting—a subject I am passionate about. And that is how this book was born—out of a desire I have had since I was 11 years old to help parents and children have better relationships with each other. I hope you get as much out of reading it as I did writing it.

CHAPTER 1

Did You Know that Your Child Has a Generous Heart?

WE WERE PACKING UP at the end of a weekend ski trip, when my daughter found a quarter on the floor of our hotel room. "Can we give it to the cleaning people for a tip?" she suggested.

"Sure," I replied, delighted she wanted to do something nice for the housekeeping staff, who I'm quite certain rarely receive positive feedback for all the necessary and yet not much fun work they perform.

As my daughter was writing *For the Housekeeper* on an envelope, it occurred to my husband that to leave only a quarter could be seen as an insult. Of course, I realized he was right.

But what if it was understood that the quarter was coming from a young child? Realizing it came from her heart might just make the housekeeper's day. I suggested she leave a note, and that she include her name and her age. She wrote:

Dear Housekeeper,
Thank you for cleaning my room. You did a very nice job.
From, Faith, Age 8

Where did this desire in my daughter to give her precious find to someone else come from? She certainly wasn't urged to do it by me. Rather, as I think back, it's clear she was *born* with a generous heart.

As we left the hotel that morning, I explained to Faith that one of the best parts of giving is the joy we feel when we imagine how good our actions will make the other person feel. Even though she wasn't going to be there when the housekeeping staff showed up in our room, she could imagine their faces when they discovered her small but thoughtful gift.

Now here's the real magic in this incident. It isn't that Faith is in any way an unusual child, but rather that her generous heart is a reflection of the way *all* children start out. It's how you and I began life. However, the extent to which a particular individual's natural capacity for generosity manifests itself depends on a variety of factors, ranging from their specific genetic makeup to their circumstances.

I believe that, above all, what influences whether a child grows up to retain the generosity that's innate is the family culture they are exposed to in their formative years.

Show Kindness When a Need Crosses Your Path

Our family had just returned from seven days of pure magic. During our cruise to the Bahamas, we had been made to feel like royalty.

My husband and I had been on two previous cruises, and on both occasions I had been deeply moved by how hard the ship's crew worked. I actually felt uncomfortable seeing how well the crew treated the passengers, knowing how difficult their daily lives had to be to make this happen. With twenty additional years of life experiences, I was prepared to feel that same discomfort on our latest cruise though I also expected it to feel a little different now that I'm a wife and a mother.

At dinner each evening, the wait staff were particularly attentive, affording us an opportunity to become quite friendly with Selvin, our head waiter. Following dinner one evening, we asked about his life. From Guatemala, he had a wife, a daughter of fifteen, and two sons who were eleven and four. For six months, he was away from home working on the ship, following which he spent two months at home before repeating the pattern. His workdays were twelve hours at a stretch, seven days a week, without a single day off for the entire six months. This had been his life for the past thirteen years.

"Why do you have to work so hard?" I asked.

"It's the only way I can provide a better life for my family," he explained.

This heart-breaking story of dedication and personal sacrifice touched me deeply, for I can't begin to fathom having to be away from the people I most love for six months at a stretch and not just for a year or two, but throughout my children's entire childhood.

"So when will you next see your family?" I asked.

"Well, it depends how much money I can save up," he said with a sigh. "This particular ship is going to be dry-docked in October, which means any crew who want to go home will be permitted to do so."

"Do you think you'll be able to make the trip?" I inquired.

"I'll have to wait and see," he responded.

Even though we had only met this man a few days earlier, he had such a sweet spirit and pure soul that it was as if we had known him forever. However, half-way through our trip, we sensed something was bothering him. Looking into his eyes and seeing the genuine kindness there, I asked what was wrong. It turned out he had only just rejoined his ship two weeks ago after two months at home, but earlier that day he had spoken with his four-year-old son and learned he was having a rough day and crying for his daddy to come home.

When Selvin choked up as he related what was happening back home, I knew in an instant what I needed to do. We happened to be pulling out of Port Canaveral in Florida, so we still had use of our cell phones and therefore access to the internet for a few more minutes before we passed into international waters. No sooner had Selvin left our table than I made inquiries concerning how much a round trip airfare would cost from Baltimore, our city of departure, to Guatemala. Once I had ascertained the price, I told my husband, "We simply have to give him an airline ticket as an additional tip so he can go home in October." My wonderful husband agreed without question.

I shared our plan with our three children and my mother-in-law, though we said nothing to Selvin. All six of us looked forward to the final dinner of the cruise, when its customary to tip the service people who have taken such great care of their guests. That final afternoon, my daughter and I wrote letters and placed them in an envelope along with the airfare. My daughter could hardly contain herself as we were seated in the dining room. Even my older son, who normally rushed off after dinner to hang out with his "cruise" friends, wanted to be there when we handed Selvin our surprise.

As dinner came to an end, my daughter called Selvin over, and I got up and walked around to her side of the table. Placing my hand on his arm, I looked into his eyes and told him how deeply touched we all had been by his story of sacrifice and dedication to his family. At this point, my daughter handed me a napkin as I started to tear up. Then, when I explained that there was an airfare in the envelope, Selvin began sobbing, hugging us each in turn, with a look in his eyes none of us will ever forget. Overwhelmed with gratitude, he told us, "I can't wait to call my wife and tell her the wonderful news." Then he asked for a photo of us all so he could show her the family who had made his trip back home while the ship was in dry-dock possible.

"It's more blessed to give than to receive," Jesus taught. Through our tears of joy on this occasion, every member of my family can attest to the joy of giving. Nothing equals the feeling we experience when we are moved to express generosity in a way that impacts someone's life in a meaningful way.

Our collective experience as a family mirrors a truth articulated by Marshall Rosenberg, an American who for many years engaged groups of Palestinians and Israelis, helping them share their fears until the hostility between them melts. Rosenberg maintained that as humans what we ultimately want is *to be the cause of joy in another.*

Kindness Is a Personal Experience

The experience of bringing joy to a family carried with it several lessons our children learned, the first of which is how transformative kindness can be.

Actually, even though I say our children "learned" this lesson, as you already know from what I've recounted about Faith and the hotel staff, it's more a matter of understanding how a family culture either crushes or reinforces what's already innate. To be generous is our fundamental nature, and the part that's learned is how to express it both meaningfully and wisely.

Many people don't take the opportunity to affect someone's life in the way we seek to as a family because they have seen how bottomless is the need in our world. Anything we do therefore feels like a drop in a bucket. Also, a lot of people give to charity, only to discover that in many cases much of their donation ends up siphoned off by administrative costs. This is one of the reasons it's so rewarding to help an individual in a direct manner. You get to share in the joy, thereby promoting a culture of kindness.

If you're tempted to think you can't make any real difference, I'd like to draw your attention to an image that sticks in my head from a story I once heard. A young woman and her husband decided upon his graduation from Princeton Seminary that they wanted to spend their lives in some place where there was great need, and so they set sail for Formossa, which is today known as Taiwan. Upon their arrival, one of their first endeavors was to talk to a government official about how they would like to help the people of his country. The official told them they were young and idealistic, but that the needs were so great, they were wasting their time and ought to go back home to America.

As the story goes, the official said to them, "Look at that ocean. If you take a bucket of water out of the ocean, it doesn't make any difference. Well, you can spend your entire lives here, and it will be like taking a bucket of water out of the ocean."

"If that's the case, I'm just going to start filling my bucket!" declared the feisty young woman, who was in her twenties. "The ocean may not know the difference, but the bucket will." Lillian Dixon lived until well over ninety, and during her lifetime established over a thousand hospitals, schools, and churches.

Most of us aren't inclined to travel to the other side of the world to help people, and neither do most of us need to. There are abundant invitations to express kindness all around us if we but open our eyes. When we see a need, if it's within our capability, it's both our responsibility and our privilege to try to meet it.

The second lesson my children received as reinforcement for their natural proclivity for kindness, and the generosity it can trigger, was that no matter where we live on this planet, as human beings we are all interconnected. In fact, in a very real sense our cruise ship was a microcosm of the world in which we live. People the world over want to enjoy life not necessarily by taking a cruise, but through the simple pleasures of home and hearth, with good food, drink, music and dance, and meaningful relationships.

Third, our children were repeatedly exposed to a

practice I consider a central facet of a healthy family culture. This practice of mine is so simple, and yet in the context of the cruise it conveyed a powerful reinforcement of the importance of being kind to our fellow humans. What was this practice? Simply that, whenever I saw a passenger drop trash on the deck and leave it for the crew to clean up, I picked it up and disposed of it in the appropriate receptacles.

I wanted our children to realize that just because the crew's job was to wait on the passengers didn't mean they were any different from those they were serving and certainly not in any sense inferior to their passengers. Even though it was their responsibility to keep the ship clean, they weren't our slaves. As passengers, each of us was perfectly capable of disposing of our own trash. Seeing the crew as our equals, it was only appropriate to return the kindness and mutual respect they showed us during the duration of our voyage by picking up whatever trash crossed our path.

Fourth, I wanted our children to know how incredibly blessed we were. Throughout our vacation, I commented often on the many ways in which we were so fortunate to be able to sail on this beautiful ship, be recipients of such thoughtful service, and visit the heavenly places at which we stopped off. Part of the culture of our family is that I never want my children to take things for granted. When we take things for granted, we deaden our natural inclination for kindness.

Life is to be savored, enjoyed, and appreciated. I think we all did a pretty good job of that on this cruise. But I wanted the children to know that wherever the opportunity arises to help someone else to savor, enjoy, and appreciate life just that little bit more, it's our responsibility to make it happen.

The greatest gift from this cruise was the joy of being able to help Selvin and his family enjoy life in a way that might not otherwise have been possible. As Marshall Rosenberg expressed, we have learned as a family that what we desire above all things as human beings is *to be the cause of joy in another*.

Kindness Is Contagious

When an article appeared on the CNN website concerning one of the year's CNN Heroes, I thought back to Selvin. The article related how Guatemala, which was of course Selvin's homeland, is still reeling from decades of civil war, resulting not only in poverty but also continued violence. Indeed, Guatemala has the fifth highest homicide rate of any country. The CNN article featured the ways in which Juan Pablo Romero Fuentes is making a difference in the lives of children in his country.

It was against this backdrop of an impoverished and strife-torn nation that I came to understand why Selvin had elected to live such a difficult life. It's why he's one of my heroes. I'm not sure I could make the kind of long-term sacrifice he's making for his family.

All during the month of October, I wondered about our waiter and whether he did in fact go home. Faith and I smiled often as we imagined him with his wife and their three children. Then, in November, we received an email telling us he and his family were having a great time together, although his visit was coming to an end. He also sent a photo of himself with his wife and children.

I realize that going home one extra time isn't going to directly change any of their lives, but hopefully it will show this family that there are caring people in the world, and in so doing evoke in all with whom they share the story a similar desire to be kind to people in need with whom they come in contact.

It makes me so happy that we were fortunate enough to be in a position to help this kind man and his family spend additional time together. My sense is that they will each magnify the kindness they received with a ripple effect, spreading it in their own unique ways. Through one small act of kindness at a time, we can all help change the world. We can create a world that reflects who each of us really is in our deeper self.

So often we teach our children by talking, talking, talking. Much of the time, we talk *at* them rather than *with* them. If we can avoid talking at them, and simply share, communicating is indeed important. And yet, I'm persuaded of the truth of the old adage that "actions speak louder than words." I've seen how children learn best by osmosis, picking up the importance of building on their innate kindness, with its accompanying desire to be generous, from a family culture.

In a nutshell, the really powerful teacher isn't what we say and definitely not our tendency to lecture. The really powerful teacher is a *way of being* practiced by the adults to whose care a child has been entrusted.

CHAPTER 2

Start a Chain Reaction With Your Kindness

WHEN ONE OF THE 110-story Twin Towers shuddered and exploded into flames, some who were trapped on the upper floors, rather than be burned alive, jumped. Caught on camera were a man and woman who leapt holding hands. What had the last word in their lives been?

Was this a confirmation that horror, pain, and tragedy ultimately reign? Or was it a heroic affirmation of the longing of people to be connected, cared for, loved?

One observer saw in the gesture of the clasped hands evidence of a mystery greater than death, a mystery that makes human friendship and solidarity possible and, in the end, triumphant. In this observer's view, our humanity is ultimately revealed as *love*.

You can see this love even in an infant. The desire to share and care comes out in so many ways. For instance, a little boy, barely able to sit upright, is given a cookie. Enjoying his cookie with a big smile on his face, he stretches out his hand to share it.

The most fundamental truth about human beings is that our deepest yearning is to be ourselves in a way that enables us to connect with one another. We want to love each other. We want to bring each other joy. Not just in the *surface* way so many of us do even in our most intimate relationships, but deeply and profoundly.

In the previous chapter, I referred to Marshall Rosenberg, who said that when a Palestinian and an Israeli finally begin to hear one another, you can see the softening in their eyes as they open to each other and love is born.

Well, the truth is that all humans want to be looked at with love, spoken to with words of kindness. We want to feel so deeply regarded that we are able to relax into this regard, comfortable with being known more completely than we yet know ourselves.

The Power of a Little Kindness

One of the worst mass murders on American soil occurred at Columbine High School in 1999, when fourteen teens were shot to death and another twelve wounded.

The first student to be killed that morning at Columbine was Rachel Joy Scott. Ironically, Rachel had recently written in her journal, "I have this theory that if one person can go out of their way to show compassion, then it will start a chain reaction of the same. People will never know how far a little kindness can go."

Rachel was so wise for her young age, and the world lost a beautiful light the day she died. Yet I contend that the light of kindness lives in the hearts of all humans, even those who appear to be the worst among us.

If this is so, why don't we see more of it? Why is our

world so strife-torn? Why do even many of our children exhibit such hostility toward one another, bullying one another sometimes to the point of causing one of their schoolmates to take their own life?

These aren't isolated cases. There's a tremendous amount of hostility between children—children who all have the same potential for kindness and caring as my daughter, and indeed who in their deepest being long to be loving individuals.

Consider that some 42% of kids have been bullied while online, while one in four have been verbally attacked more than once. Some 35% of kids have been threatened online. That's every third child. About 58% of kids and teens have reported that something mean has been said about them or to them online.

Although official statistics of the American Justice Department show that one out of every four kids will be bullied sometime in their adolescence, other bullying statistics show that some 77% of students admit to being the victim of one type of bullying or another, while Bureau of Justice School statistics tell us 46% of males and 26% of females have been victims of physical fights. The situation is so awful that, each day, 160,000 kids don't attend school because this is where they are bullied, teased, or harassed.

These statistics represent a huge amount of hostility. And yet, I contend they don't represent the real nature of our children. They show what children are like when something has gone seriously wrong with the family, society, and culture in which they are growing up.

Where Does Hostility Originate?

I once heard the story of a Hindu saint who, while visiting the river Ganges to take a bath, came across a group of family members who were shouting in anger at each other. Turning to his disciples, he asked, "Why do people shout in anger at each other?"

The disciples thought for a moment, then one of them said, "Because we lose our calm, we shout."

"But why should you shout when the other person is just next to you?" probed the saint. "You can as well tell the person what you have to say in a soft manner."

The disciples offered several answers, but none proved satisfactory. Finally, the saint explained, "When two people are angry at each other, their hearts distance a lot. To cover that distance, they must shout to be able to hear each other. The angrier they are, the stronger they have to shout to hear each other to cover the growing distance."

The saint went on to inquire, "What happens when two people fall in love? They don't shout at each other. They talk softly because their hearts are close. The distance between them is either nonexistent or small. The more they love each other, what happens? They don't even speak, only whisper. Finally, they don't even need to whisper. They simply look at each other, and that's sufficient."

I was putting away laundry when I heard my husband shout down the stairs, "Brady, you have until the count of three to come up these stairs!"

I stepped out of my closet and went to investigate. At the top of the stairs was a dad who was irritated that our seven-year-old had ignored him when asked to put away his laundry. When my husband raised his voice because he had been ignored, it sent our son running for the hills.

I gently intervened by asking Brady in a quiet voice to please come upstairs. When he reluctantly honored my request, I began talking to both my husband and my son about what had just transpired. First, I asked my husband, "How did Brady's ignoring you, then running down the stairs when you shouted at him, make you feel?"

"I was angry," he admitted. When I asked what exactly he was angry about, he explained, "When Brady ignored me, it made me feel bad and then I felt sad."

With this information, I helped Brady see that instead of just trying to avoid the situation with his dad, he needed to understand the negative effect his behavior had on their relationship. Then I asked both of them how this situation could have gone differently. As the discussion proceeded, I could feel the tension dissolving between them.

We had twenty minutes before we needed to move on to our next activity. Since Brady likes to race the clock whenever we are involved in an activity, I asked him if he thought we could all finish our laundry jobs in eighteen minutes, whereupon he instantly ran to his room to start putting away his clothes.

What delighted me most was when my husband called after him, offering to help him hang up his shirts— something he normally does. I disappeared back into my own closet to complete my chores. Several minutes later, a broad smile spread across my face as I heard squeals of delight as my husband and son wrestled on his bedroom floor.

Later that evening, when my husband and I reflected on

the laundry incident, I pointed out that his anger with Brady had resulted in emotional distance between them, which was mirrored in the way Brady ran downstairs to avoid dealing with his upset dad. Healing of the rupture occurred when Brady understood that his dad didn't just feel angry, but deeper down felt sad. This realization brought understanding, drawing out Brady's compassion and thereby building a more meaningful connection between them.

In such situations, what often happens is that parents yell louder, demanding action. The child is eventually forced to comply, which leads only to resentment and a feeling of disconnection. Yes, the job gets completed, but at what cost to their long-term relationship?

Compliance can never be the goal of effective parenting. Connection is the goal. It may take a little more time to address an issue more consciously, but the investment is well worth it and will pay dividends for both parent and child.

The unpleasantness in our home that afternoon, and how we resolved it, was a practical demonstration of Rachel Joy Scott's assertion that if one person takes the trouble to go out of their way to show compassion, it will start a chain reaction of kindness.

When Kindness Gets Amplified

If we apply this insight to a broader landscape, the difference between a little girl who wants to give away her quarter to make someone else happy, and a child who says mean things about another on Facebook, is that one feels connected to their kind heart, whereas the other feels disconnected.

I maintain that to the degree that a child is connected to their own loving center, they will wish to be kind to their peers instead of bullying and hostile.

Thankfully, when Rachel's loving heart was silenced at Columbine, her message of showing compassion and kindness wasn't silenced. On the contrary, it got amplified.

To honor her dream, Rachel's dad and stepmom created rachelschallenge.org, a nonprofit that has so far reached more than 21 million people. The organization has received over five-hundred unsolicited emails from kids who attended a Rachel's Challenge program in their school and who, when they contemplated suicide, decided to reach out for help instead of ending their life. Children who felt disconnected and in despair discovered within themselves a desire to connect.

Perhaps even more indicative of the kindness at the heart of every human being is the fact that those who said they would stand up for a student who was being bullied went from 35% before the Rachel's Challenge program was presented in their school, to 78% following the program.

These kids tapped into their caring heart, the part of all of us that intuits we are inherently interconnected and thrives on both expressing and being a recipient of kindness.

CHAPTER 3

Understanding the "Problem Child"

ADOPTIVE PARENTS I WORK WITH shared with me their frustration with their fourteen-year-old daughter. The adoption had been finalized only three months earlier, but they were already seeing behavior that was upsetting to them although to me it was entirely understandable.

Their teen was not only becoming distant, but she also more and more expressed a desire to be with her biological mom, even asking if she could spend Thanksgiving with her. Naturally, this made the adoptive parents sad. Hurt, they felt unappreciated.

I suggested that adoption is rather like marriage, which is the way their adopted daughter explained it to me about two years ago when we were discussing the possibility of her adoption. It's a long-term commitment and, in a way, a forever kind of commitment. This makes it scary. In an adoption, it's normal to get cold feet the same way brides and grooms often do leading up to their wedding day.

The situation was complicated by the fact that this young lady was behaving like a pendulum, swinging between closeness to her biological mom one moment and disconnection from her the next. In the center of these frequent swings sat the two adoptive parents, hoping they were where the pendulum would eventually come to rest.

The reason adoption had become necessary in the first place was that the birth mother was simply incapable of caring for her daughter. You can imagine the negative feelings this young girl experienced toward her mother when she was told she was going to be sent away to be adopted.

However, as I helped this young lady work through her feelings of abandonment, she came to see that her mom was acting in her best interests by giving her up for adoption. Moving beyond accusations of betrayal, her heart opened to the point she was eventually able to forgive her mom.

As the pendulum swung away from the adoptive parents, they found themselves feeling left out in the cold. What do a couple who have taken a child into their life do in such a heart-rending situation?

My goal was to help them not to take their daughter's actions personally. Instead, they needed to realize this was a natural process the child needed to work through. Gradually, the adoptive parents settled into a place of acceptance, waiting patiently to see where the pendulum would finally come to rest.

What Acceptance Really Means

Acceptance isn't the same as resignation. When we are resigned to a situation, we resent it but put up with it for a greater good. Acceptance goes beyond this.

When we accept, we no longer resent what's happening, no longer seek to control it, and don't withhold whatever participation on our part might prove beneficial. Instead, in the way this couple did, we embrace what's transpiring as part of a necessary process in the individual's evolution as a person.

It's important to grasp the fundamental difference between resignation and acceptance. With resignation, we "sort of " accept something, since it's being forced on us and we have little choice. But in our heart, we're opposed to what's taking place and if we can, we try to hurry it along, hoping to "get it over with."

Where there's resignation, we are still attached to our idea of what the outcome of a situation ought to be. We want to impose our will on the other and regret the fact we have to keep silent. It's as if we're saying, "You can do it, and I won't stop you since you're set on it. But don't expect my blessing."

If you examine this attitude, which so many at some time or other take toward their children, it's not only unkind, it's sadistic. It's a sharp arrow aimed to hurt. To utter such a statement, we have to have deadened our natural kindness.

How to counteract the tendency to be unkind, even sadistic in that we want to punish the person, when the child we love crosses us?

Acceptance requires detachment from our emotional investment in the situation. We are no longer focused on *our* feelings, *our* concerns, *our* needs. The issue becomes entirely a matter of what's best for the other party. We move beyond seeing it as a question of our personal wellbeing and happiness.

When acceptance is genuine, we can choose to take a step that can be truly life-changing for everyone involved which is exactly what this couple did. Because they were able to detach themselves from whatever the outcome of the situation might turn out to be, while in no way detaching themselves from their adopted daughter in terms of caring about her, they were able to give her the incredibly selfless gift of not only allowing, but actually encouraging, an ongoing relationship between the young lady and her biological mother.

In this situation, the child is able to benefit from the best of both worlds. She is being raised and cared for by two loving, stable parents, while at the same time she gets to maintain a connection to her biological mom, who also loves her deeply despite the fact that her own unresolved issues mean she can't care for her adequately on a daily basis.

Detachment Facilitates Profound Connection

Detachment, sometimes referred to as non-attachment, strikes at the heart of our tendency as insecure human beings to want certainty, and therefore to try to control the outcome of things.

I need to point out that the concept of detachment is often greatly misunderstood, as if it meant we either don't have feelings or squelch our feelings. Quite the contrary, detachment which is an insight that comes to us from Eastern philosophy is precisely what allows us to become profoundly involved and deeply caring.

When the young lady who was being adopted began going through this highly stressful and horribly confusing process, she couldn't detach emotionally from the many voices in her head that told her such things as:

"My mother doesn't want me"

"My adoptive parents are taking me away from my mom"

"I can't trust anyone—I will always be betrayed."

The thoughts that pass through our head when we are in a situation of this kind trigger strong emotional reactions. Life becomes painful not only for ourselves but for everyone involved.

In therapy, this young lady began to understand the situation in a much more realistic way, which enabled her to simply observe the thoughts that came to her instead of believing them and reacting to them. As she did so, her emotional swings subsided. In time, she was able to accept her mother's limitations without blaming her and without telling herself that her mother was giving her up for adoption because, as a daughter, she was either unwanted or unlovable. Detaching from her troubling thoughts and volatile emotions, she found she could now connect to her adoptive parents *and* her birth mother.

The ability to feel deeply is fundamentally different from a strong emotional reaction. One is grounded in reality, the other in the things we tell ourselves, which are often irrational and have little to do with the actual situation.

Feelings certainly can generate emotion, but they are much deeper than the volatile emotional reaction we may have to a situation. Indeed, our real feelings may be 180 degrees opposite from an emotional reaction, as the young lady's case demonstrates. Reacting to the thought she was being abandoned, she pulled away from her mother emotionally. Yet her real feeling was one of wishing she could connect as, when she understood the facts of the situation, she was in due course able to do. Similarly, instead of pulling away from her adoptive parents because, from an emotional point of view, she saw them as taking her away from her birth mother, at a deeper level she was able to feel connected to them and make a home with them.

The abiding peace that arises in us when we are able to detach from having to control a situation is a balm to hurting souls. We can actively love a person, holding nothing back without any guarantee they will love us in return. This is possible because we have become sufficiently grounded in our *own* inherently loving center that we no longer need the other to reciprocate in order for us to feel good.

In this particular case, the adoptive parents were able to love their daughter without taking ownership of her unsettling behavior. Not reacting to her shifting moods enabled them all to begin the journey of drawing close, since they were no longer afraid of being hurt. Were hurt to come, they knew they would be able to soothe themselves and be at peace.

The Goal of Parenting Is Differentiation For Child *and* Parent

In Western psychology, the Eastern concept of non-attachment is sometimes referred to as "differentiation." Developed by Murray Bowen, the concept goes beyond what we generally think of as individuation.

To be an individual in our own right to find our own way in life, based on our unique genetic makeup and particular bent is a vital aspect of growing up. To become individuated is to learn that, while we always want to take other people into consideration, happiness is fundamentally about being *true* to ourselves.

To be individuated means we don't betray ourselves by bending to the will of others in order to placate them, and in the process violate our own integrity. Indeed, the best way to please others in the long-run though not necessarily in the immediate situation is to make sure the way we conduct our life is pleasing to *us*.

Individuation is only one side of the coin, the other being differentiation, which is about learning to function together in such a manner that we can be true to ourselves while also allowing others to be true to themselves.

To become differentiated entails things like rubbing up against one another in our families, relationships, and place of work. It's in the nitty gritty of our everyday connection that we learn how to be true to ourselves while also honoring others. A differentiated person is someone who is grounded. They won't compromise themselves, a topic we'll return to in a later chapter. They will negotiate, but from strength instead of always being ready to capitulate to keep the peace.

When there's conflict, differentiated individuals don't become reactive—don't take their toys home. Instead of either exploding at the other person or, conversely, distancing themselves, they can stay connected. In fact, when we become truly differentiated, we don't even get nicked by a difficult exchange with someone, let alone wounded, because our sense of who we are is in no way dependent on how others feel or act toward us.

Now, with this background, allow me to make a statement that may be surprising to some. The adoptive situation I've been describing would normally be seen as a difficult problem to solve. For many, it would constitute a major crisis. But what I'm proposing is that it's an ideal setup for the various parties to develop differentiation.

We are all much more resilient than we realize, but this capacity has to be drawn out of us. So along come situations that test our metal, as if life were teasing out of us what we're truly made of.

Once you begin to see a difficulty you are having as a parent with a child whether your biological offspring, adopted child, or a child you are fostering as an opportunity to develop a more differentiated sense of yourself, you'll handle it entirely differently. In fact, you'll start to look for all the ways in which the situation is inviting you to become in everyday reality more fully who you intrinsically are.

Instead of seeing a difficulty, you understand you are being given an opportunity which is exactly what happened in the case of this adoptive couple as well as the teen with whom they were sharing their kind hearts.

CHAPTER 4

Getting to the Root of Bad Behavior

A SET OF FOSTER PARENTS with whom I work discovered that their fifteen-year-old foster son was doing poorly in three subjects in school. He had failed to turn in several homework assignments in various classes, and he was earning poor grades on exams. Naturally, the parents were upset at this news. Fearful that the child would grow up to be a failure, their initial inclination was to lash out by punishing him in the hope of bringing him under their control. To them, it seemed evident that if he wouldn't do it himself, he needed to be *forced* to bring his grades up.

It never occurred to these foster parents, as it doesn't in so many similar cases, that the child was presently incapable of what they were asking of him.

I pointed out that any attempt to control this child would backfire by causing resentment. Children may hide their real feelings when they are punished, since they don't wish to lose their caregiver's love, but resentment is an inevitable reaction to all forms of punishment. This is because, even though parents may tell themselves they are doing the child a kindness, children intrinsically sense that there's nothing kind about punishment.

"What really needs to happen in this situation is to get to the root of the dysfunction," I explained. "Behavior of this kind always reflects the child's sense that he's somehow disconnected from life, which includes the adults in his life."

Due to the child's age and the fact this was his first placement in a foster home, the couple had indeed struggled to connect with him. For this reason, my focus as their coach was to search for and identify ways they might establish a meaningful connection.

This young man was a very good baseball player and loved the game. Driven by their fearful reaction to the child's failure to perform well in academics, the foster parents decided that if he didn't improve his grades significantly, he would no longer be allowed to play baseball.

Their plan was to refuse to sign the boy up for the spring baseball league in their town. If this didn't do the trick, they would then take the matter further by calling on the coach of his high school baseball team, explaining that even if he made the team, they wouldn't allow him to play unless his grades improved to where they wanted them to be.

Do you imagine the boy in any sense interpreted these threats as kindness on the part of his foster parents?

Thinking Through the Consequences of Our Decisions

My first task was to help these foster parents think through the consequences of their actions. Would intervening to prevent the child from playing baseball lead to good feelings between them, or to hostility and a desire to disconnect? And what might the consequences be in terms of the boy's involvement in the life of the school? Would he feel more closely connected to his academic subjects, or more distant from the whole idea of school?

I pointed out that this young man was only in ninth grade, so the baseball coach had never even seen the boy play. Calling the coach about his grades would put a black mark on the young man from which he might never recover as far as baseball went. The effect of this on the boy's self-esteem, not to mention his ability to develop a social life among his schoolmates, could be catastrophic.

Such a punishment would likely also backfire in another way. Having come from a tough background, this ninth grader had found the one thing in life he truly loved. To have this jerked out from under him would be devastating, likely causing him to lose all hope of finding fulfillment in his life.

Hadn't it been enough of a struggle for this young man to have to deal with not living with his parents, without depriving him of his one great passion? Mightn't he begin to see life in terms of one deprivation after another? And what would denying him access to his passion teach him about the adults in his life?

I explained to these foster parents that when an issue of

this nature arises, before anything else, it's essential to believe that just like all children at heart this boy wanted to do well. The fact he wasn't doing well in several classes was a reason to look deeper to figure out what was causing him to fail.

To get these foster parents thinking along lines other than taking away baseball, I put forward several suggestions. Did the boy perhaps have a girlfriend who might be distracting him? Might he be enrolled in classes that were too difficult for him? Was he having such a hard time being away from his parents that he didn't care about how he was doing in school? Or maybe he was struggling with adjusting to the different atmosphere of high school?

The possibilities for the boy's malaise were many, and I simply wanted to open these caregivers up to become curious about what might be going on in this young man, thereby offering them an alternative to struggling to control his behavior out of fear he was going down the wrong path.

A reorientation of our thinking of this kind requires us to believe that all children truly want to do well. When they aren't doing well, something is preventing them from doing so. It then becomes our job to discover what's holding a child back, and to figure out how we can help them break through that barrier.

This is a radically different approach to parenting from believing a child is inherently "bad" or wants to do poorly. It involves a major paradigm shift in terms of our thinking.

The Centrality of Connection

We sat down with the young man and I explained we all believed he had a lot of good qualities. I assured him we knew that, deep down, he wanted to do well, but that it seemed something was holding him back. I promised him we would do what we could to help get to the bottom of his quandary.

I also helped him understand that his foster parents wanted him to do as well as he personally was able to do. This might mean he earned a C, or it might mean he made an A. The grade itself wasn't important. All his foster parents cared about was that he was being true to his capabilities.

In a situation like this, it needs to be realized that a child who has experienced disappointment after disappointment may not even know what it means to "try his best." Such a child has likely never had an experience of his best. This is why supporting his interest in baseball was important. He didn't need further beating down, further deprivation. He needed to be patiently inspired so he might develop a little *hope* in life.

Because the foster parents had already threatened him with the loss of baseball, it was necessary to address this directly as a way of giving him hope. I assured him their intention had been good, and that they just wanted him to be okay in life. No one wished to prevent him playing baseball, and I made it clear that the threat had been a last resort. As he saw that we all wanted him to enjoy his chosen game, I watched his resistance dissolve before my eyes.

For me, the key was to get this young man thinking about how he could do his best. This is such a different approach from the threats so many foster parents and parents issue based on their fear that a child won't do well. Fear can perhaps jolt someone into action for a time, and I understand why caregivers resort to it, which is often out of a feeling of desperation. We hope to shock our children into performing as we expect them to.

Especially with foster children, it's easy to expect the worst and parent from a place of fear. But to suspect a child of being a "problem" based on our fears, coupled with whatever evidence we may have seen so far of a behavior problem, is the *least* helpful approach we can take.

Children who have already been removed from their home harbor lots of negative feelings about family life, their new circumstances, and especially themselves. Even when this isn't the case, fear is never a healthy motivator over the long haul. Kindness, which alone can open up their heart to the wonder of being alive, is the route forward.

Why Threatening Children Is Counterproductive

Why isn't instilling fear of failure or of punishment in a child effective?

Well, for one thing, it has a clenching effect. Blood pressure rises, heart rate quickens, muscles tense, and we sweat (to name just some of the physiological changes we go through). Such bodily reactions are extremely valuable if you're in an Australian billabong and you see a crocodile move off the bank and into the water toward you. Fear can also be an asset if you startle a poisonous snake that's in your path when hiking the Rockies and stop dead in your tracks instead of blithely proceeding. And, too, a little fear can be a lifesaver if you live in the forests of India and a man-eating tiger is seen lurking around your village at night.

To see why fear has its place but is counterproductive when it comes to getting a child to do their homework and pay attention in class, it's helpful to understand a little about how fear arises.

The human body is equipped with two essential nervous systems, generally referred to as the central nervous system and the peripheral nervous system. Via the spinal cord, the central nervous system transmits information from all of our bodily functions to the body's control center, the brain.

A division of the peripheral nervous system, known as the autonomic or visceral nervous system, is tasked with the particular function of pepping us up or slowing us down. It can do this because the autonomic nervous system also consists of two branches, which we call the sympathetic and parasympathetic nervous systems.

In everyday jargon, we speak of getting pepped up or slowed down as "fight or flight." The effect of triggering the sympathetic nervous system is to mobilize us, whereas triggering the parasympathetic system dampens things down. We might equate our sympathetic nervous system to a car's accelerator and our parasympathetic to the brake.

When we're afraid, our autonomic nervous system goes into overdrive. Under threat, to be able either to defend ourselves or run can save our life. However, if our mode of everyday existence is one of fear, whereby our sympathetic nervous system is constantly revving our engines even as our parasympathetic is simultaneously pressing hard on the brake you can imagine the energy we draw down from our reserves and the enervating effect this has. There's not much left for creativity, excitement about learning, or aligning our actions with the highest values.

If a child lives under the dark cloud of a belief that, if they don't behave in a certain way or live up to someone else's expectations, they will be scolded, deprived of something they value, or lose a privilege they enjoy, their autonomic nervous system is going to wear them down. Now the child who was once excited to explore everything from a caterpillar on a leaf, to a worm crawling on the sidewalk, becomes someone with little enthusiasm for learning.

Many foster kids in particular have little experience of a life that's shown itself to be benevolent toward them, and they are therefore especially short on inspiration and enthusiasm. When we scare kids who have already been through a rough time by uttering threats to deprive them of the little they still find exciting and actually enjoy, our intent to get them to open up to their potential and become more expansive in their approach to life backfires. Instead, they are likely to close off even more.

Restoring a Child's Enthusiasm for Life

When a child's joie de vivre has been deadened, what needs to happen is for a caregiver to identify those areas of the child's existence in which there's still a spark of life.

Then, we build on these aspects, gradually coaxing more and more of the vast acreage of deadness in the child's interior, caused by perhaps years of neglect or abuse, back to a state of productivity.

As a child's enthusiasm for initially even just one aspect of their day, such as baseball, increases in response to our encouragement, we establish a beachhead of nurturing, opening up an avenue of authentic contact the child can trust. In this area, if not in others yet, the child feels our kindness, and in response their heart begins to open to us, even if just a little at first. The trick now is to feed this instead of opposing it.

In other words, what's called for is the exact opposite of threats, disciplinary action, and punishment. Stoking the fires of enthusiasm with kindness and support is the way forward. Not pushing, which has more to do with our agenda than the child's own internal agenda, but providing a supportive atmosphere in which the child's inherent enthusiasm for life can expand and flourish.

What's happening, without even any conscious effort to bring it about, is that the child is beginning to experience what it is to be listened to, what it feels like to have someone actually pay attention to them for the individual they truly are. This is the crucial piece when it comes to assembling the jigsaw of a restored meaningful life. It's the lynchpin in what can seem like an extremely puzzling conundrum in which we don't see a way forward with a particular child.

Connection, wherever it can be established by genuine listening, is paramount. In any trying situation, it's always the way forward, even when it may not appear to yield any immediate tangible results. Which is, of course, why injecting fear into a child's life is counterproductive, since fear causes the kind of clenching that leads to a disconnect.

If, at our core, we are riddled with self-doubt, we will project this negativity into every circumstance in which we find ourselves. This is what's happening when a child gets labeled a "problem." It isn't that the child is inherently a bad person, but that they color everything from the perspective of the bad things that have happened to them.

Whether we are parents, foster parents, caregivers, teachers, social workers, or therapists, our job is to connect with the children in our life in such a way that we help them believe in themselves. For at its root, malaise in all its expressions is ultimately sourced in a failure to believe in ourselves, and therefore a lack of trust in the goodness of life.

Getting to the Root of the Problem

If we are to oust fear from our child rearing toolbox, thereby opening the door for connection, we are going to have to address our own fears. As long as we as parents or caregivers are coming from fear, it will be impossible not to resort to tactics that generate fear in a child.

For this reason, staring down our own fearfulness with a faith-filled heart is vital. When we have the courage to do this, we pave the way for a spirit of heartfelt connection to flourish in every contact we have with a child which is the *only* thing that can truly move a parenting, fostering, caregiving, or therapeutic relationship forward.

The simple fact is that if *we* don't have faith in ourselves, we will find it hard to believe in others and we certainly won't trust that the universe is our friend. Such doubt will then contaminate every interaction with the children in our life.

No child can overcome their difficult circumstances and thrive without trust—without believing in themselves and the importance of their place in the scheme of things. To set a tone of believing in ourselves, in one another, and in life itself is the foundation of effective parenting.

As caregivers, it's therefore essential that we recapture our own original trust in life. Along the way, we too developed a measure of distrust of life and disbelief in ourselves. I doubt anyone is free of this phenomenon, which we might well name as our "original sin." It isn't badness that's the root of the human problem, but a failure to believe in our essential goodness.

How, then, to restore an atmosphere of trust? How to foster an unequivocal belief in ourselves and those over whom we are given charge?

It so happens that the family is the ideal setting for doing just this. Indeed, there's no better context for confronting our own self-doubt and self-deprecation than in the presence of a child who doubts themselves and expresses this self-doubt by acting out!

I'll go beyond saying that it's the ideal setting. It's the perfect *setup*, if we can but recognize it, for drawing out the faith we ourselves have abandoned along the way in our own journey of growing up for to one degree or another, the faith in ourselves we come into the world with has been eroded in all of us by a self-doubting society.

How a child's initial faith in themselves, in us, and in life itself can be nourished in practice is the topic to which we now turn.

CHAPTER 5

Bring It Out into the Open

EACH SUMMER, my best friend from childhood and I get together. I look forward to spending time with her, and it was particularly exciting when she came with her daughter to spend a few days in our home.

Having said this, it's also the case that if our eyes, ears, and hearts are open even the most enjoyable of occasions often turn into moments of insight, reflecting back to us some aspect of how we can so easily not be truly available to connect with our children.

The first night, when my friend was putting her daughter to bed, I also put Faith to bed. We have a bedtime ritual, but because I was so thrilled to be able to talk to my friend, I was in a hurry to get through the routine.

Much of what we communicate is accomplished nonverbally. Consequently, my daughter picked up on my desire to rush her off to sleep and began resisting me leaving the room—something she doesn't usually do. Becoming frustrated, I reminded her in an exasperated tone that my friend was here visiting and I wanted to spend some time with her. "Surely you can understand that?" I said, sounding annoyed.

At this point, Faith grew sad. In a quiet voice, she explained that she really wanted to spend some special time with me, though she understood I needed to go downstairs to be with my friend, whereupon I bolted out of the room.

No sooner had I left than I realized how poorly I had handled the situation, especially since Faith is a particularly sensitive little girl. Not only is she sensitive, but she's wise, which meant that had I explained the special circumstances, she would have understood what I needed that night.

Now here's the irony of it. My friend fell asleep putting her daughter to bed, so we didn't end up spending time together after all! I had upset my daughter for no reason.

The following evening, I determined to rectify the damage I had done. At bedtime, I confessed to Faith that I felt badly about how frustrated I had gotten the previous evening, and that I was unhappy with how I had handled the situation. "You're such a wise little girl," I said, "that had I simply explained that I wanted to spend some time with my friend since I don't get to see her often, I know you would have understood."

The incident illustrates where much of what we think of as a child's "bad" behavior originates with how we don't truly communicate with them. She had become clingy the previous evening only because she picked up on the fact I had an unstated agenda that was undercutting my sincerity in the way I related to her. I had made her feel guilty for wanting my attention, when all that was needed was authentic open communication.

After all, Faith knows about spending time with friends. She loves to spend time with her own best friend, and I do everything in my power to allow that to happen as often as possible. My daughter is such a feeling child that she told me she felt sad for me that my best friend lived so far away and I didn't get to see her often. To cap the conversation off, she said, "You don't need to spend so much time in my room tonight. You should go downstairs and spend this special time with your friend. I'll be just fine."

My friend and I ended up only watching half a movie before we both realized we were too tired to finish it, though it was nice just to be able to relax together without any guilt over rushing through the bedtime ritual because Faith and I had communicated honestly, stating our needs plainly.

The lesson is that when we don't become fully present with each other but have an undercurrent of a personal agenda, a bunch of clutter crowds in on the situation—power struggles, guilt-trips, impatience, and a lack of presence. Clear communication, stating exactly what we need or what we mean, keeps the focus on the real issue, which avoids triggering any kind of acting out.

Bedtimes Are a Setup!

Bedtime can be one of the most challenging aspects of raising a child, particularly as the child grows older. It's also a wonderful opportunity to learn the importance of authentic, open, honest connection.

My daughter began complaining that a bunch of her friends get to stay up later than she does and asked me why she had to go to bed so early. Rather than plunging headlong into a disagreement about bedtimes, I explained that those who stay up later probably no longer get to enjoy the elaborate bedtime routine she and I enjoy. Our bedtime story, talk time, and snuggle time usually takes about forty-five minutes.

Instead of laying down the law, I told her that, as a child grows up, it's completely normal to transition to a shorter bedtime ritual. Then I asked, "Do you want to think about switching to that sort of bedtime? You'd get to stay up later playing, but we wouldn't spend as much time together in your room."

She thought about it, then decided that although she wouldn't like to engage in a new routine every night, she wouldn't mind trying it a few times to see how she liked it. With this decided, she happily drifted off to sleep without another thought.

A few days later, when I asked whether she wanted to try the new bedtime ritual, she responded positively and stayed up later. But when it was time for bed, and I told her I would go up and tuck her in, after which she would simply go to sleep, she suddenly wasn't at all excited about the idea. "Can you stay in my room for a little while and read me a bedtime story?" she asked.

"It sounds like you're reconsidering whether you're truly ready to move to an 'older kid' kind of bedtime," I suggested, to which she agreed, going on to explain that she still loved when I read to her, talked to her, and snuggled with her. She simply wasn't ready to let go of this routine, which I verified was also quite normal. Then I read her a very short story and snuggled for just a few minutes, for which she was grateful.

I want to point out that I didn't treat this as a teaching

moment, which is what many parents might be tempted to make it. In a situation of this kind, it's crucial to sidestep any tendency to make it a teaching moment. There was no reason to deprive Faith of a little attention when she realized she had made a choice that wasn't in accord with her preference at this stage in her journey.

The exchange my daughter and I went through was part of the normal developmental process, not something to be turned into some kind of "lesson," which it's easy to do if we allow our agenda to get in the way of connection. It's not a disciplinary approach that's called for as our children explore what it means to grow up, but kindness, which affirms a child's trust in life's goodness.

Life itself becomes a child's teacher if, as long as there isn't an issue of safety involved, we have enough trust in the process of growing up to step aside. In this instance, had I resisted my daughter's request to stay up later, this would likely have led to a power struggle, followed by resentment of what she might then interpret as a desire to control her. At the other extreme, I could have shamed her for still needing such an elaborate bedtime routine at her age, which would have undermined the natural progression of an age-appropriate shift from dependence to interdependence.

Instead, I shared with her what I felt was happening, not only with herself but also with her friends. As a result, rather than the message getting lost in a battle between mother and daughter, she was able to see the situation for what it was—entirely a matter of whether she was ready to move to a slightly more independent phase of her development.

Clearly she wasn't, although I also knew her well enough to understand that connection with others, especially me, was so very important to her—so much so that she was able to fall asleep only after she felt all was right in her little world. It's this feeling that builds a child's trust in themselves and in life in general.

About a week went by before I asked Faith whether she wanted to try the later bedtime, with its shorter routine, again. She said she wasn't ready. We agreed to put the idea on the back burner until such time as she felt she wanted to move forward on this.

Forcing children's development is counterproductive. It always comes back to bite us in the butt in the teen years or beyond in the form of some display of dysfunction. Each stage of growth must be initiated by the child, engaged in fully with our support, and only superseded by the child's own desire when their innate wisdom tells them to move on.

Our role is to be there for them, providing an atmosphere of kindness that nurtures their spirit and facilitates their flourishing at whatever stage they find themselves to be.

CHAPTER 6

When Mistakes Are Made

WHEN I RECEIVED A CALL from our middle school's vice principal, I wondered why she would be calling me. No doubt it was to follow up on the meeting my neighbor and I had with both herself and the principal to discuss the school discipline policy and how we might improve the climate of the school. The furthest thing from my mind was that she might be calling to inform me of an incident involving my seventh grader.

It turned out that one of the boys at the school had said something inappropriate to my son, who then repeated it to his classmate, only louder. Overhearing it and imagining the comment was directed at her, a female student went to the office to report what had been said to the vice principal.

Learning of what had been said, I was at once shocked and embarrassed. Thankfully, I had an hour to process my feelings and figure out how I would handle the situation before my son was due home. I had always told him that if he got into trouble at school, I shouldn't have to find out from someone else. On the contrary, it was his responsibility to tell me. To honor what I had taught him, I decided not to bring the matter up, but to give him the opportunity to do so. I confess it was difficult for me to bide my time, though I realized it was essential I do so.

When he arrived home from school, Noah came straight into the kitchen and placed a detention form in front of me for my signature. "What happened to earn you a detention?" I inquired, making sure my voice was calm.

As he proceeded to tell me the story, I realized he felt entirely comfortable coming to me about his predicament. Over the years, I had worked hard on not overreacting when things like this happen, focusing on understanding my triggers so that I could short-circuit any temptation to "lose it." Because Noah had come to know this about me, he always felt free to share a problem he was experiencing, as well as to own up to a mistake.

Just as I suspected, Noah didn't know the meaning of the inappropriate word he had used. This opened the door for an in-depth discussion of the word and the context in which it might appropriately be used.

With the meaning of the word now clear, I continued, "Your dad and I have worked hard to raise you to be a gentleman, and gentlemen don't use inappropriate words like this around females. From all I can see, you usually conduct yourself like a gentlemen, right?"

"Yes," he replied.

"And you want to be seen as a gentleman?" "I do," he affirmed.

"So, as a gentleman, how do you think you should handle this situation from this point on?"

"I already apologized to the girl," he said. "Although she really didn't understand why I was apologizing, since she said she only heard the other boy say the word, and it was him she reported, not me. She was surprised when I told her I got a detention."

Evidently when the male student was called to the vice principal's office, he told on my son for repeating the word, even though the young lady didn't hear him say it. Since both boys said the word, I wasn't going to make an issue of the fact they had both been given a detention.

"I'm delighted you apologized to the girl right away," I confirmed. "Do you think you also ought to discuss the matter with the boy?

It turned out that Noah already planned to tell the boy he wanted to be left out of conversations of this kind in the future, since he didn't wish people to view him in that way. I agreed it was an appropriate thing to tell this student. Then I asked, "Is there anything else you might need to do to make amends for this inadvertent mistake?"

"I don't think so," he said.

"What about the vice principal? Should you apologize to her?"

"I don't want to do that," he replied. "I didn't do anything to her." I agreed with his assessment that an apology wasn't needed, though I felt he needed to say something to her because, since she was the school disciplinarian, I had found myself in an awkward position when the vice principal called me. After all, only a few weeks earlier, I had told both the vice principal and the principal that my son wasn't the kind of student who would ever earn a detention.

"I can understand why that would feel embarrassing," Noah agreed.

To conclude our discussion, I further explained that

many students who bring a detention form home find themselves being punished. Their phone gets taken away, their video games banned, or they find themselves grounded and not allowed out with friends. My son understands I don't believe in punishing him, and that all that was required was for him to make full amends for what he did.

Following our conversation, he sat down at the computer. When I later read what he had written, it was a perfect response to the situation. "I had a talk with my mom and understand the full severity of what I did," he wrote. "I have apologized to the people it affected and I'm going to think before I speak next time. Normally, I hold myself to high standards and I will give 100% effort to make sure it doesn't happen again." It was short and to the point, and it pleased me greatly.

I once heard Dr. Shefali Tsabary, author of *The Conscious Parent*, suggest to parents that, in any dealings they have with their children, they might ask themselves, "At this moment in time in my interaction with my child, am I building connection or furthering disconnection?" It's a really pivotal question, going to the heart of what it means to parent well.

In my interaction with my son on this occasion, it was clear from the way he didn't feel at all hesitant about sharing his mistake with me that we had already established a strong connection. Our discussion, followed by his response to everyone involved, was further testimony that I was building connection by handling the situation in this manner instead of in the usual way parents punish their children, often without ever really hearing them out. I could feel the connection. In fact, I could tell how connected Noah felt to me throughout the evening as we went on with our activities.

Punishment, yelling, harsh words—these are a recipe for resentment and disconnection. If we want to raise ladies and gentlemen, we have to treat our children gently. Kindness, understanding, and working on solutions together is so much better than generating hostility by being mad at them.

How Consequences Accomplish What Punishment Can't

Seventh grade was also a time when my son developed a bad habit of not bringing his book bag home from school. It started out innocently enough, leaving it in his locker on Fridays because he had no homework over the weekend. Then, since he has a proclivity for "systems thinking," this morphed into not bringing his bag home on any of the days he had no homework, which miraculously seemed to be frequent in seventh grade (not that I'm complaining!).

I didn't have an opinion on my son's book bag choices and could certainly understand his point. Since he walked home from school, why carry a heavy bag when he had no work to do?

Then, when he was going to bed one night, I sat in Noah's room while he finished brushing his teeth. When he returned to the room, he remembered he had a form I needed to sign for school. "Can you do it when you leave my room?" he suggested.

Hmm. I wasn't about to take on the responsibility of remembering to sign a form after we'd spent time together and I finally went back downstairs. "I'd much prefer you go get the form now," I replied.

When he went downstairs, he realized he must have left his book bag at school. It could even be outside, where he was throwing a football around with his friends after school. Having got out of the routine of bringing his bag home, he clearly no longer paid any real attention to it. It was now that I began to understand why he should bring it home as a matter of habit.

There followed a domino effect. Several chilly mornings, Noah had worn pants over shorts to school, then left the pants in his locker when he went to gym class. But because he wasn't bringing his bag home, the number of pairs of pants in his locker was multiplying.

As it happened, we had engaged in a discussion about the dwindling pairs of pants in his closet several days earlier because I wanted him to understand that, if he ran out, we weren't going to run out and buy him new pants before he went off to school on the morning this occurred. If he intended to continue leaving his book bag at school, he needed to figure out a plan for bringing home the pants that were in his locker.

Whenever an issue arises with my preteen, I always handle it by talking it over with him and helping him figure out a way to solve the problem for himself. I've found there's no need for dishing out punishment, lecturing, or getting angry. Following our conversation, as he always does, he figured out this pants problem. He stuffed them all in his book bag that day to bring them home, together with the paper I needed to sign. Except that this happened to be the day he didn't notice he had left the bag somewhere. Now we had a dual problem—no paper *and* no pants.

I've learned the importance of using few words, especially with a pre-teen, only those required to convey the message. This was no time for discussing solutions pertaining to the future, let alone for lecturing. What to do?

It was 9:30 p.m., so I asked my husband to drive Noah to school, where, despite the fact it was pitch dark, hopefully they would find his book bag. A half hour later they returned with no book bag, perhaps in part because the flashlight he had taken wasn't a good one. At 10:00 p.m., he and I set out with two better flashlights. I let him know that if we couldn't locate the bag, he would be leaving for school thirty minutes early the next day to search for it in daylight. This wasn't punishment, just a natural consequence of his actions.

We searched the field from one end of the school to the other. As we did so, he retraced his steps, meticulously describing to me everything he did on his way home from school. Still, we came up empty.

Despite being irritated by the book bag incident, I couldn't help but be impressed by how well my son self-regulates in terms of the time he gets to spend with his friends. He was in the habit of bringing his football to school every morning so he and his friends could play catch after school as they moseyed home. This helped them release pent up energy from sitting in classes all day.

The one other place my son thought he could have left his book bag was in the office. The day before, his friend had taken Noah's unlocked bike to the lost and found, thinking he had left it there by accident and walked home. It turned out he was actually staying after school for basketball and hadn't forgotten his bike. So after school today, he had called in at the office to retrieve his bike. Might this be where he left his book bag?

After searching the grounds, as we came around to the front of the school, I noticed that the custodian was still there. When I rang the doorbell, the very kind man came to the door and let us in to search for the bag. When we entered the office, there it was in the lost and found. It was then that my son realized he had put the bag down on the floor as he tried to maneuver his bike out of the office, then forgotten to retrieve it.

Arriving home, he put all of his pants in the hamper, and I signed the form for him. Then, even though it was 10:30 p.m., my husband and I sat down with him to talk about the domino effect of his choices. I mentioned earlier that he's what I call a "systems thinker," which enables him to see the entire picture and identify the cracks in any given system. Consequently, it was pretty easy for him to grasp how leaving his book bag at school had failed him.

"I need to bring my bag home every day, even if I don't have homework," he announced as our discussion moved to a conclusion. Being out of the habit of feeling the weight of his bag on his back, leaving the bag in the office hadn't set off an alarm as he rode home on his bike. He also realized that not bringing his book bag home daily had meant he'd had to wear pants that were too short for him earlier in the week.

Let the Situation Teach Its Own Lessons

Consequences are powerful teachers, and the beauty of allowing them to play out is that they don't cause a child to resent the parent. Earlier in my parenting career, I would likely have doled out punishment for a mistake of this kind, since it had so affected our evening. This might have entailed loss of phone privileges, denial of screen time, grounding—all the usual ways we tend to "discipline" pre-teens.

I might well have yelled, threatened, shamed and I certainly would have lectured. I could also have made Noah pay for all the pants he left at school out of his allowance. Plus, I could have refused to help him find his book bag, since it was his problem after all, right?

Had I used these tactics, and had they actually succeeded in prodding him to bring his book bag home with him every day, at what cost would this have been achieved? He would have missed out on the opportunity to become intrinsically motivated to bring his bag home—in other words, to be *self*-disciplined and thus increasingly self-reliant.

Worst of all, he would have resented me, telling himself what an awfully mean mom I was, which would have deflected his focus from the real issue—the fact that, by abandoning his routine of carrying his bag home, he was making a choice that wasn't in his best interests. And what would have transpired the next time he forgot to bring his bag home? More punishment, more yelling, more lecturing, more shaming?

In the end, what would all of this have amounted to?

Less connection, when what I work so hard for and that's so crucial, especially at this age is increased connection.

The awesome thing about this story is that the entire time my son and I were looking for his book bag at school that night, instead of feeling resentful, perhaps even furious, I felt connected to him. I was literally walking alongside of him as he tried to solve his problem. This is exactly what parenting asks of us—to walk alongside our children.

These days, the book bag comes home every single day. Not only have I never had to remind him about it, but he hasn't forgotten anything else important at school. And all of this was accomplished without resorting to punishment, yelling, lecturing, or shaming. Because no emotional energy was siphoned off into resentment of his parents, my son's focus stayed on simply doing what serves him best—bringing his book bag home.

I see my most important task as the mother of a pre-teen, and a parent in general, as standing beside my children, supporting them as they learn how to make choices that will help them be successful in life. Sometimes I have to supply more support, as when we searched for the bag at night and sought the help of the janitor, and sometimes less.

But at all times, whatever the circumstances, I'm my children's chief cheerleader.

CHAPTER 7

Building Connection that Endures

WHEN OUT OF THE BLUE ONE DAY, my daughter asked me what Poppy's voice sounded like, I found myself tearing up. "Well, I can let you hear it for yourself," I told her. Then, retrieving an old video, I popped it into our one surviving VCR. (How technology advances!)

My dad was the kind of person who was handy, which meant he loved to putz around with tools fixing things. He was also organized and knew where things were. Ever since his death, whenever I go into my garage and can't find what I'm looking for, I silently ask him to help me find the item. Every single time I've made such a request, within minutes I've stumbled upon what I was searching for. Whether he actually hears and in some magical way heightens my awareness through the universal field that connects everyone and everything, or whether it's that I shift into more of the kind of consciousness he exuded around such things, isn't important. It's the heart connection that matters.

Some of my fondest memories of my parents revolve around the years we shared Thanksgiving. This past year, I was getting set to brine the turkey for the family gathering the next day when, rummaging in my kitchen, I realized the turkey wouldn't fit in any of my pots! Following a minor moment of panic, it came to me that I possessed a larger pot we used for camping. Phew! I could brine the turkey after all.

Except that, when I set foot in the garage and couldn't find this monster pot that, I now recalled, I used every Thanksgiving for this purpose, it dawned on me I had donated it to our church yard sale during the summer.

When a feeling of panic again began to arise, I paused. "Dad," I whispered, "I could sure use your insight right now." Moments later, it came to me that I still possessed my parents' crab-steaming pot. I pulled down the ladder that led to the loft and mounted the stairs. Sure enough, there was the pot and when I hauled it down and filled it with brine, the turkey fit with room to spare. (We are from Maryland, so if you know about Maryland and crabs, you will understand.)

This happens every time I ask my dad for help. I should have thought of this that evening when we couldn't find Noah's book bag. The point I want to make is simply that, in some mysterious way, our loved ones are always with us. We may appear separated when they die, but only a thin veil hides us from each other.

What to Do When You Feel Disconnected

I always think of Thanksgiving as a joyful season in my life, a time when I'm full of gratitude for the many blessings in my life.

So when I was feeling out-of-sorts one Thanksgiving morning, even a little sad, my husband surprised me by reminding me that I usually go through a period of sadness around this holiday. When I paused to think back, I realized he was correct. I guess I had developed a habit of blocking it from my memory.

It was close to Thanksgiving, November 30th to be exact, when my father died. Growing up, we always hosted Thanksgiving dinner. Mom got out her fancy dishes—the same ones I now use—and she and I left dad to busy himself setting the table at its most elegant, along with bringing up extra chairs from the basement to seat the additional family members. Dad was always so excited about our family coming together that he gave himself a stomach ache! Of course, I knew it came from a place of deep love and joy.

With the dishes out of their storage and dad in charge of the table setting, mom and I retreated to the kitchen to watch the Macy's Thanksgiving Day parade, which was our custom on this day, as we mixed and stirred and poured. It was an occasion that always inspired the warmest feelings for me, since it was inextricably woven together with my fondest memories of my parents.

This particular year, I had thought about mom and dad all through the week leading up to Thanksgiving. The thoughts were happy memories. When the actual day arrived, every plate I pulled out, I thought of dad. Every dish I prepared, mom was on my mind. That's how the sadness started.

By midday, I was feeling so sad that I had become snippy with my husband. As I grew grumpier, I noticed how my mood was rubbing off on him, and he in turn had begun snipping at our kids. This was the wake-up call I needed.

I stopped what I was doing and turned my focus inward. When I did so, I realized that, despite the years that had gone by, my grief over the loss of my parents was rearing its head. This was no way to enter into Thanksgiving dinner with our extended family. What could I do to make myself feel better?

When I shared what was going on inside me with my husband, he confirmed that he had sensed sadness about my parents lay behind my grumpiness. "It's why I've been trying my best to make everything perfect," he said. "It was the only thing I could think of to help make you feel better."

I pondered this for a moment, then explained, "When I feel sad, I don't need perfection. I simply need to be allowed to feel sad. It's the fact I've been trying to avoid the sadness because Thanksgiving is a happy day that's the reason I've been grumpy."

When we find ourselves becoming emotionally reactive, we need to identify the feeling that's behind the reactivity. Then, by giving ourselves permission to experience it fully, we integrate it, which allows the energy locked up in it to become fuel for living a more deeply feeling, deeply connected, deeply loving life. It's when we avoid a feeling, trying to stuff it down, that it morphs into an emotional reaction we are probably going to act out as I was doing with my grumpiness and snippiness.

Before I could feel better, I needed to allow the grief to move through me. But how, when I was busy preparing

Thanksgiving dinner for our family and guests?

I had about an hour until our first relatives were due to arrive. I decided I would take our dog for a short walk. This way, I could be alone with my feelings. Besides, being out in nature has a way of rebalancing me. I guess it restores the sense of being connected to reality as a whole, including my parents even though I could no longer visibly enjoy their company at the Thanksgiving dinner table.

When I reentered the house, I still wasn't feeling as buoyant as I had hoped I would, so I let my husband know I was going up to our room for a while. Sitting down in our walk-in closet, I told my parents how much I loved them, how badly I missed them, and how much I wished they could be here with me.

I happened to open my eyes just as our dog and cat were both entering the closet to be with me. Sitting there in silence with them, something about their presence brought comfort to my aching heart. Breathing deeply, I became very still, allowing the sadness to wash over me, through me, and out of me. Now at last I was ready to enjoy Thanksgiving with my family.

Children Intuit What We Are Feeling

Before I noticed what was going on earlier that Thanksgiving day, my sensitive daughter picked up on my sadness and tried in a variety of ways to comfort me asking me questions, rubbing my back, inquiring how she could help.

"I'm just sad, but I'll feel better soon," I said, fobbing

her off, even though I realized what I was telling her was far from satisfying her.

When I was at last feeling better, I took Faith aside and explained what had transpired that morning. She was familiar with the need to address sadness directly by allowing ourselves to feel it fully, since it's a skill I'd taught her. Now it made sense to her why I had gone for a walk, and why I had then sat alone in my closet for a time, allowing only our two pets to keep me company.

Children learn from us more by osmosis than anything. My daughter had picked up on my sadness, watched me struggle with it unsuccessfully, then saw how I had been able to integrate the grief I was experiencing by making space to experience my feelings fully rather than trying to escape them or mute them.

Alone in my grief, I had been able to allow my tears to well up and flow freely. It occurs to me how different this is from the way many of us deal with our children's tears. When they are upset, if their crying continues longer than a few minutes, we tend to become uncomfortable. I've heard so many parents, anxious to end the crying of a child at all costs, threaten, "Stop your crying now, or I'll give you something to cry about." I wonder how we would feel were the adults in our lives to react to our tears this way?

Once I had explained what had been going on with me that day, my daughter looked into my eyes, told me how much she loved me, hugged me tight, and went off to play.

Lessons Learned, Lessons Imparted

I'm blessed to live the kind of life in which my family life and my work feed into each other, the one enriching the other. Lessons learned, difficulties experienced in my home life spill over into the way I help others with their families.

Raising children effectively takes ingenuity. Indeed, I'm persuaded that to bring a child up to be a worthy contributor to society is the single most challenging task we ever undertake. But if there's a single key to addressing behavioral issues, it's surely the lesson I learned that Thanksgiving, which is to look deeper than the presenting problem and locate the root of the pain. To pull this off with three very different children, I've had to learn to really focus on the message beneath the words, beneath the behavior. As a therapist and parent coach working with foster, adoptive, and biological families, I've had to teach other parents to do the same.

On one occasion, I found myself with a little girl of four who had been having a difficult day. Fighting constantly with her two-year-old sister, and not listening, she was being generally defiant. While the foster mom was telling me this story, the little girl got into yet another fight with her two-year-old sister, which triggered a timeout.

Ostensibly, the fight had occurred over books. So when the timeout was over, the foster mom explained to the four-year-old that she must share the books with her sister—that it wasn't fair for her to have eight books, whereas her sister had only had one.

This all sounds reasonable, right? After all, it's certainly important to encourage children to share.

However, it's also important to expect of children only what they are capable of in terms of their age, as well as to take into consideration the particular dynamics that may be going on not only within the child as an individual but also within the family as a system.

While the foster mom was talking to the little girl, I asked if I might chip in. Explaining that her foster mom and I had noticed she was having a rough day, I asked, "Is there something that's bothering you, perhaps something that's making you sad?"

The little girl immediately burst into tears, whereupon she climbed into her foster mom's lap and sobbed for a good five minutes. As this was going on, her foster mom held her, rubbing her back to comfort her as she did so.

I explained to the foster mom that, in this situation, crying was actually good for the youngster, since it allowed her to release the pent-up charge she had in her little body as, indeed, crying had been good for me when I found myself missing my dad that Thanksgiving morning. Comforting the little girl in the way the foster mom did was also extremely helpful, since it affirmed that the little girl's feelings were valid and not something to be ashamed of or hide away. As I was explaining this, I noticed that the child had stopped crying and become interested in what I was saying.

Since I had her voluntary attention, again I asked whether something was making her feel sad that day. In this welcoming atmosphere, where she could see that we truly wanted to understand, her response was instant. "Yes," she confided, "I miss my other mommy." Whereupon tears once again began flowing.

It was amazing to see this little girl have so much insight into what was bothering her, and we went on to talk about how normal it is when a child is apart from their other mommy to miss her and sometimes even feel really sad. I explained that talking about how we are feeling, and sometimes crying about it, helps us feel better.

"You know, when you are feeling sad, you can tell your foster mom," I affirmed. "The two of you can talk about it, and she can help you to feel better. That way, you won't end up fighting with your little sister, then having to sit in timeout." The little girl liked this idea and said she would do it. During the remainder of the evening, she didn't get into a single fight with her sister. On the contrary, she was happy and smiling, along with dancing around the room as she played. It was beautiful to watch.

The real gem from this incident is that the foster mom, who was quite savvy when it comes to kids, had from the beginning been pretty sure she knew what was bothering the little girl. The problem was that, instead of going straight to the root, she found herself waylaid into dealing with the surface behavior the child was presenting— something many of us tend to do. Deflected from the main issue in this way, her efforts had all been directed not to the root but to stopping the behavior it was triggering.

I liken this to weeding. If we want to get rid of a weed, we can't simply pull its leaves off. We must dig down to the root and extract it, lest the weed simply grow new leaves, spread its seed, and thereby become pervasive.

By becoming aware of what was really going on with this little girl, we were able to isolate the cause of the behavior and address it head-on. Even at the tender age of four, this youngster was able to understand what we were talking about and felt so much better for being heard, understood, and seen in the light of what she was dealing with.

Whenever we find ourselves reacting to the members of our family, or children are reacting to one another, we need to excavate the roots of the emotions that are arising. There's always a reason we are crabby, grumpy, critical, angry, or controlling. Once we identify it, we can integrate it so that it troubles us less and less and so that the energy locked up in this negative emotion becomes available for positive feeling and action.

By growing alongside each other, openly sharing the journey of becoming the person we are with the rest of our family in an age-appropriate manner, we all benefit. We are drawn closer, so that the house in which we live becomes a true home—something really worth giving thanks for.

CHAPTER 8

Be Kind to Yourself
Get a Life of Your Own

AN ISSUE MANY MOMS especially struggle with is a clash
between their natural desire to do something creative—
something different from changing diapers, preparing
meals, and running their children to after school activities
and their duties as a mom.

All of us have a need to engage in creative endeavor for
our personal enjoyment, as well as to feel we are
contributing to the betterment of society. We may also have
a desire to engage with other people who are interested in
our particular area of creativity.

The problem is, pursuing an activity of our own, quite
separate from being a mom, generates a feeling of guilt in
many of us. And, since we're out of the job market, we
may not know how to go about fulfilling our wish to be
creative.

If you happen to be a reader of South Jersey MOM
magazine, you've probably come across some of my
articles. They began appearing in the December 2014 issue.
I want to tell a bit about how this came to be. My writing
for publication is all about wanting something and going

after it.

I had been aware for a while that, in addition to coaching parents, which I absolutely love, I also wanted to be a writer. Something about the writing process allows me to clarify and focus my thoughts in connection with my parent coaching. I've actually written for much of my life, and now I found myself wanting to move to the next level.

An urge came to me to Google every local parenting magazine and send an email to the editors. "I want to write a monthly column for your magazine," I told them. Many never replied. But one of the editors—it only takes one! — got back in touch with me, which led to a lengthy phone conversation, the outcome of which was that I was asked to submit my first article.

Because the magazine comes out only once a month, I knew I could work this into my existing schedule without adding stress. In fact, because it would bring me much joy, it would ameliorate some of the stress that accompanies lacking sufficient creative outlets.

While I was discussing the project with the editor, she confided, "I had another parent who wrote for me over a considerable period, and it so happens she discontinued her column. For the past several months, I've been hoping the right person would come along to fill this mom's shoes."

It may seem I contacted this editor out of the blue and got lucky. However, I believe there's more to it than luck. Whether we're talking about gravity, a magnetic field, or how light waves behave, on the physical plane there's a certain way things operate in the universe. What I and many like me have come to see from our personal experience and insight borne out also by the Great Wisdom

66

Traditions of many cultures is that it's not just in the material realm, but also in the head and the heart that things have a way of functioning that, if we align with it, can work for our benefit.

In my particular case, on this occasion I felt the inspiration to put myself out there as a writer just when this magazine editor needed someone like me. I don't mean to imply there's an imaginary "person in the sky" who's pulling strings—nothing of the kind. But, just as when iron filings come within the reaches of a magnetic field, they have a way of lining up in particular patterns, I've become convinced there's a creative field at work in everything—a field that generated, and continuously lures to higher levels of self-expression, this whole shebang we call the universe.

The Way the Universe Works Also Works with Children

There's a difference between controlling and influencing. The feel is different, as is the effect.

The creative process expressed in the evolution of the universe with its myriad of galaxies and planets, followed by the development of species here on at least our own planet if not many more, has been one of fields of attraction operating within the four essential forces of the universe, blending their magic in a creative symphony.

This evolutionary epic is unfolding in its own way. No one's controlling it—it's in many ways a random process in which mutations resulting from quantum phenomena are then selected for the conditions extant in a particular environment. "Time and chance" play their parts, as wise King Solomon said. Yet infused within the process is the lure of increasing beauty, order, centeredness, harmony— the results of an underlying intelligence at the heart of every quark, photon, quantum fluctuation, and field.

We know today that the creation is all of a piece. It's a universal fabric in which we are each individual ripples. Even forces such as gravity are now being understood in terms of distortions in the fabric of space-time.

As the great wisdom traditions have long pointed to, and many of us experience in everyday reality, the creative influence that connects us all is present in all aspects of our daily reality and it's this that welled up within me as a creative urge, inspired me to reach out, and in due course attracted an editor receptive to what I had to offer.

There's a parallel here with how bringing up children works best. When we control our offspring, forcing them along our chosen pathways for their lives, we override the natural intelligence of the universal creative impulse that seeks to well up in them in their own special expression of its creativity.

Helping my own children, along with the children I work with in adoptive and foster situations, find their unique way of manifesting their essential being, so that I can help draw it out and thereby influence them in the direction that's right for them, frequently challenges my creative reserves. This is the case not only when it comes to addressing dysfunctional behavior, but also in seeking to inspire them to expand their interests and explore their potential.

However challenging it may be to draw out a child's

natural zest for living meaningfully, I am persuaded that we must take up the challenge and not resort to control. By prescribing our children's path for them, we cut the legs out from under them, so that they are left with no opportunity to walk their own path. In a very real sense, we are torpedoing their evolutionary role in the tapestry the universe is weaving.

This doesn't mean we can't exercise a strong influence over our children. It's a matter of working with their inherent inclinations rather than attempting to impose our way on them. I saw this particularly vividly in connection with a famous children's author's birthday.

Each year, the school my nine-year-old attends holds a book fair to honor Dr. Seuss' birthday. What a gift Dr. Seuss was to all of us. He blessed us with so many enjoyable books and is one of my favorite children's authors. During the week-long event, at bedtime one evening, my seven-year-old and I cracked up taking turns reading *Fox in Socks*. It was delightful watching him belly laugh. I'm thankful my children have all grown into young people who love to read.

It so happens that when he was younger, my twelve-year-old didn't enjoy reading. In fact, I worried and stressed over his inability to enjoy books, and along the way I tried a variety of techniques to ignite that spark in him. When they all failed to motivate him, I despaired of what to do.

When he was in third grade, it occurred to us that it would be a real treat to take a family trip to Disney World in the fall of our oldest's fourth grade year. As we pondered this possibility, it occurred to us that there might be a way to get a little extra mileage out of the venture.

On New Year's Day of third grade, we offered Noah the chance to "read" our family to Disney World. We live a thousand miles from Orlando, so we told him that for every hour he spent reading, he would earn ten miles. If he earned all one-thousand miles by October, we would go to Disney World.

Noah bought into this idea instantly. We had read him book one of the Harry Potter series in kindergarten, but hadn't gone further because it seemed too scary for his young age. As soon as he returned to school after the winter break, he brought home book two, and the rest is history. He devoured the remaining six books of Harry Potter, then went on to read *Percy Jackson and the Olympians*, followed by every other book Rick Riordan had written.

Between February and August of that year, Noah plowed through thirteen books the size of Harry Potter. To this day he continues to be a voracious reader. It was all down to finding a genre he enjoys. Today, reading is one of his favorite pastimes, something for which I'm thankful. I know how important reading is to success in school, as well as to attaining a rounded education for everyday life.

Looking back, I realize there was no need for me to stress over this the way I did. I know now that it was fear-based, which is never helpful. What good could it do to keep going over questions such as, "What if Noah never grows to love reading? What will become of him?" Though the stress was very real at the time, it seems quite silly when I think back to it from my present perspective. Isn't most of our worry about "how my child will grow up" rather silly?

My husband and I thoroughly enjoy reading, and the simple fact we modeled it for our children was likely to rub off on our oldest sooner or later. Other than modeling, all we did was find a way to encourage his willingness to *try* a book. Once he actually got into it, he realized he loved reading fantasy. Modeling a desirable lifestyle, but then allowing children to invent their own version of the principles we model, is our most powerful teaching tool.

The really important lesson to take away from this is that if children are going to do something in a sustained manner, their motivation needs to originate internally. Parents facilitate this when they simply prime the pump but don't force the flow. As far as reading goes in our family, the only work we have to do as parents is to exchange books at the library when our children finish what they are currently reading.

Just as fantasy is what worked to get Noah into reading, feeding his imagination and therefore both his creativity and his enjoyment of life, the iPad and similar gadgets have induced some children who have resisted books to delve into eBooks. It's a simple matter of recognizing not only how different our interests are, but also the different ways in which we learn. There's no fixed way things have to be done, and what works for one may not work for another.

How much better it is to invite self-exploration, influencing our children by encouraging them to become a clone of no one—not us as their parents, not their teachers, and not their peers—but to develop according to their unique bent. In this way, we work with the creative flow of the universe instead of damming it up

It's beautiful when you observe the world working in

this way and I believe it works this way all the time, if only we have the eyes to see it. But we have to let go of control and the urge to dictate, and instead become receptive to what arises within us in the form of our desires, as well as responding to the opportunities with which life presents us. They are there in far greater abundance than we imagine.

Listen to Your Inner Longings

A friend in another part of the world experienced a catastrophic natural disaster that swept away his home, his career, his savings, and most of his friendships. A heartbeat from retirement age, his life felt washed up. At his age, no one would want him in his chosen profession.

When he shared his plight with the one or two friends who remained in the region, the suggestions they had for how he might support himself caused him to feel like he was dying inside. They may have seen how he could reinvent his life in one of these ways, but to him it was as if he was up against a brick wall.

An impulse kept coming to him. It was something he had always wanted to do, and yet it seemed an impossibility, especially now in his depleted state and shrunken circumstances. When every door seemed closed to him, except the one or two that felt deathly in terms of his interest, he finally simply became still. He stopped talking to others about his predicament and began listening within himself.

No voice spoke to my friend, other than those repetitive voices we all at times hear in our head—voices that in his case exacerbated his dire straits by predicting he was doomed to life in a grotty one-room apartment with an income adequate to support only a bare subsistence, not to mention nothing creative to do with his days.

In the absence of an inner voice to direct him, there came a "knowing"—that's the only way he knew how to describe it. He shared with me that he had been touched by the story of Elijah in the Hebrew Scriptures. He resonated with how this spiritual teacher had become washed up, so discouraged as to want to die.

When Elijah appealed to God for help, the response was that he had to journey to where he was completely alone in a wilderness, and there the divine would reveal itself. In that location, all alone, he first encountered a huge lightening storm, so great that it generated a firestorm. Yet there were no answers for him in the firestorm. Next came a mighty wind, no doubt a tornado that ripped rocks apart. Still there were no answers. Finally, a huge earthquake shook the region. In all of these displays of the power of nature, there was nothing to give Elijah the guidance he sought.

It was in what happened next that Elijah found his answer. The traditional translations say there came a "still small voice," but they fail to capture the force of the Hebrew. The New Revised Standard version gets it right: "There came a sound of sheer silence." It was in this sheer silence, this utter stillness, that the divine became known.

And that's what happened to my friend. No voice, no internal debate, no answers from friends—just a knowing, deep within, that this was his time to do what he had long wanted to do.

At such moments, we know in a wordless, intuitive way. It's something we really can't bring into conscious thought and analyze, or we lose the essence of it. Yet it's present in the background, characterized by a deep peace. We just know.

Let me caution that if something has a "charge" to it, it's probably coming from your thoughts or an emotional neediness or drivenness, in which case it isn't the knowing of which I'm speaking.

The sound of sheer silence in which there is a wordless, intuitive knowing is fundamentally different from what many look to for guidance—experiences such as a tummy tuck, a warning light, a red flag. Usually these are based in fear, which is of an entirely different order from the peacefulness of the sound of sheer silence. Anything we propose doing that goes contrary to our existing brain patterns is bound to generate red flags and gut feelings. As a deeper consciousness seeks to break through, it has to rewire our neural pathways. To see how this works, if you haven't already done so, watch the movie *What the Bleep Do We Know?* sometime, where how the brain's pathways can be rewired to better align with our soul's desire is beautifully illustrated.

Responding to his heart's desire as I did with my writing, my friend picked up the phone and reached out to a source that seemed utterly unlikely to be interested in him and yet it somehow felt so right. It took a couple of calls, spanning a six week period, for the person on the other end to confide that she had been looking for someone with precisely the talent my friend had to offer. A decade later, he's loving the experience of expressing his creativity.

Is there something you would like to bring into your life—something originating not in goals your parents might have thrust on you, nor in the aspirations of others, but from your own silent center? An activity you've been wanting to take up, a career you'd love to pursue, a change of location that resonates with your heart? Perhaps there's a hobby that speaks to you, or a friendship you'd like to develop? Not something at the level of thought or emotion, but from deep within your center where you are one with the pulsating desire of the intelligence that has birthed the galaxies.

If this is your experience, what's stopping you? Perhaps you aren't at a point where you can take a huge leap, but maybe you can take a tiny step closer to living the life you dream about. I guarantee you it's worth it.

Will You Be Depriving Your Children?

A great concern many parents have is that if they follow their dream, they will deprive their children of their presence. They hold back on the creative endeavor they long to follow because they don't want to neglect their family.

When we follow the whims of our emotions or the thoughts regarding what it means to be a success implanted by others during our upbringing, we often do end up neglecting our offspring. We're away on our project when we ought to be providing them with a meal or tucking them in bed. Our absence registers deep in their psyche, leading to a feeling of emptiness that may well haunt their lives for years to come and, because of their unmet neediness, wreak havoc in their relationships.

However, when a dream we are pursuing originates from the harmonizing creativity of the universal intelligence of which I've been speaking, it has a way of balancing out our life in a manner that's beneficial for everyone concerned. Because it springs from love, it doesn't trade in neglect or deprivation. It uses inspiration to foster self-development, deep connection, wholeness, and fulfillment.

If, instead of being driven by an inner itch of neediness we're attempting to scratch with external accomplishments, we are being directed from the flow of bounteous goodness at the heart of reality, we will always find ways to adequately meet the needs of family.

I use the word "adequately" advisedly, for when it comes to parenting, many of our cultural norms major in indulgence of our children, our spouse, our partner, our parents, or other significant individuals in our life. We are so oriented to catering to the needs of those who make demands of us, constantly trying to please them and keep them happy, that we lose ourselves in the process.

Neglect is indeed a terrible thing in a child's life, robbing the child of the kindness that nourishes self-esteem, self-development, and the feeling of being connected to the whole. A child may be scarred for life by serious neglect.

But equally—and far less understood—many of us create an unhealthy dependence in our children and others with whom we share a close relationship. We foster not self-development, which involves a growing self-reliance, but material and emotional fusion, to the point that our lives are so enmeshed that none of us understands where the other leaves off and we begin. Our lifestyle, our moods, our goals are controlled by the expectations of others, as well as by our reliance on them to "be there for us" in every imaginable way.

I've spoken already, in an earlier chapter, about a healthy "walking alongside" our offspring in the parenting journey. Our relationship with a child doesn't begin in this way, for the child is at first utterly dependent on us for its sustenance. But the aim of the arrow should always be toward the target of interdependence, whereby we are available when necessary to help one another, without creating an unhealthy dependence by which the other's wellbeing revolves around us.

When we are attuned to the deep stillness at the heart of our being—the same stillness at the core of the whole of reality—it will offer us opportunities to make our life meaningful that will also enhance the lives of others. Never does it detract. But such enhancement may, by society's often highly enmeshed expectations, appear to be depriving the other of something. What that "something" may be, if we are truly coming from the stillness of being, is a deprivation of using the other as an emotional or material crutch so we can avoid having to experience the frequently challenging and sometimes painful task of growing up into our own unique person.

Too much involvement in a child's life will damage a child's psyche every bit as much as too little involvement. Children are inherently resilient, and our parenting needs to draw out this resilience instead of undercutting it. To accomplish this, we must find the balance between supporting and nurturing on the one hand, and gently pushing a child away from needing us, toward independence, on the other. Only in this way will we get to the place where we can walk alongside each other.

How Fulfilling Your Dreams Will Help Your Children

There is an ingenious, creative, artistic center in all of us. But unfortunately the standard methods of parenting have a way of shutting us down to this inner urge to express ourselves. For this reason, the parent who dares to follow their heart becomes the key to unlocking in their children what society has worked so hard to lock up.

We have spoken about how children learn more by osmosis, which involves participating in the culture established in a family, than from any amount of preaching on our part. In no area of life is this more the case than when it comes to unleashing our originality, innovativeness, resourcefulness, and desire for creative self-expression. It's seeing these qualities enacted in our lives, without any attempt to force them onto our children, that most fuels a child's development.

The aim of effective parenting isn't to prod a child, but to inspire a child. Pushing and prodding originate from our own neediness, which generates a fear in us that our children might fail. When we engage in urging instead of inviting, we undercut the child's own propensity for self-development. If we would restrain ourselves when we become fearful, simply providing a climate in which a child might flourish by living in a creative manner ourselves, the child would in its own manner and on its own schedule discover what flourishing means in its unique case.

Sadly, society—especially the educational system—believes that pushing a child is essential for the child's future. This is solely because we have a fixed idea of what success looks like. And so countless young minds are schooled in traditional ways that subvert their natural inclinations. Is it any wonder so many end up in jobs they find boring, their performance mediocre, and their natural creativity untapped?

Somehow we must learn that desire is the driving force of life. So often scorned as "unspiritual," mistaken for greed or lust, desire suppressed is precisely what precipitates greed and lust. For while desire springs from a sense of our worth, and longing to express this in some worthwhile endeavor, greed and lust are the product of the neediness that results when our natural desire for the fullest expression of ourselves is crushed.

We tend to think that when we desire, it's because we lack what we desire. But to the contrary, desire is a sense of fullness at our center that seeks expression. We desire because we want to express ourselves, not because we feel empty and lack something. As an insightful British author once put it, "Desire is love trying to happen."

The Buddha rightly identified craving of which greed, lust, jealousy, envy, impatience, and the like are symptoms as the root cause of human suffering. Craving comes from the belief that our lives are empty. It's driving force is neediness, characteristics of which are clinging and grasping.

The difference between craving and authentic desire is that when we crave something, we want to use that object or person to complete us, which is fundamentally different from wanting the object of our desire in its own right. For instance, people want to use another for sex, but they often don't want the person. They want the prestige of a certain job, but they don't actually relish engaging in the work. Hence desire isn't about acquiring, but about wanting to be more—to know and experience ourselves more deeply, more fully.

My move into writing for a monthly magazine was an act of self-love, a response to a desire that involved a "stretching" of myself, an expansion of the way I understand myself and currently experience myself. In allowing myself to be stretched, my very being was coming alive. And when we permit this to happen in ourselves, we simultaneously invite it indeed, encourage it in our children, who by osmosis pick up on the fact that this is what the journey of life is all about.

What this comes down to is that when we are kind to ourselves and respond to the deep currents of the heart, we are kind to our children. Yes, dad may have to help them with their homework tonight as we attend a meeting. Or they may have to manage the math or the essay on their own, assuming they are old enough to take on such a responsibility! In this way, our allowing ourselves to be stretched also stretches them. Not an overstretching, which won't happen as long as we stay attuned to the universal field that connects us, just adequate stretching to spur their growth.

Where's Your Trust?

Many parents I'm in touch with come from a place of fear when it comes to stepping out to live more fully. They are afraid of what might go wrong in their children's lives if they take up a hobby or, perish the thought, a career! But if we are to allow our heart's desire to guide us, all such stretching of ourselves, and in turn of our children involves an element of trust.

Playing it safe is actually the unsafe way to approach life, because it fails to draw out the resilience each of us possesses innately, which alone can equip us for life's challenges. If there's one thing we can be sure of, it's that life will throw us curves. No amount of protection we can offer will save our children from having to deal with such curves. A successful traversing of life's journey requires us to find within ourselves, and help our children find within themselves, the resources to cope with those events that test our metal.

I am persuaded that Freud got it wrong when he interpreted life in terms of satisfying our basic hungers. That's only the beginning, the ground level. What life asks of us is so much more, involving an ascent into the heavens. Desire is about "coming to be" in everyday life what we are in an ever-unfolding manner discovering to be our potential. It involves an infinite fullness actualizing itself, in the process teaching us what we are capable of.

To take such a journey requires trust in ourselves, in our children, and in the basic goodness of life. It involves a sense that the universe is on our side. Or, said differently, that life itself is fundamentally kind and intends the very best for us. But this "best" can only be realized to the degree we are willing to exercise faith in ourselves and actually step out into pastures new.

Now this may stretch you a bit, but I need to share it anyway. It's an important, indeed pivotal insight and once we allow ourselves to thoroughly digest it, it enables our trust to soar. The fact is, your kids are going to make a lot of mistakes in life. As desire wells up within them, it's going to get short-circuited along the way, so that they fall prey to greed, jealousy, envy, lust. They'll think they want whatever particular object, person, or experience has caught their attention, and they'll attach themselves to it sometimes with disastrous consequences. But falling down in this way, failing to allow desire to stretch us and instead take the form of a "latching onto," is part of how we awaken to what it is to be a desiring being.

If, then, your teen becomes obsessed with a particular boy or girl, whereupon their heart gets broken because the attraction either isn't reciprocated or doesn't endure, your task as a parent is to be a calming presence while the child works through the pain and grief.

Notice, I didn't say we need to talk in such situations unless this is invited. I said we need to be a presence. It's our trusting presence that will invite our children to remain open to their desiring center, instead of closing up to avoid the pain of future disappointment. For it's when we close up to our heart that we stop short of wanting the person and become a user of people, wanting only to the point that we scratch our own itch.

The central fact to keep in mind, especially in the traumatic teen years, is that just because our children make mistakes doesn't render *them* a mistake. It's this vital truth that can keep our trust in them alive. If we don't make a big deal out of their mistakes, but allow them to work through them in an atmosphere of trust on our part, they will learn. After all, the only things we really learn are those we learn for ourselves.

The crises of life aren't an attack on us. They don't come because life is against us. On the contrary, they are what invite growth. When a crisis strikes in our children's lives, our task as parents is to be there providing a trusting atmosphere in which they can work through the crisis for themselves. It's crucial to keep in mind that it isn't what we say that inspires their confidence to do so, so much as the vibes they feel emanating from us. If, behind our words of encouragement, we are fearful at heart, our children will pick up on this no matter what we say, just as a horse can spot a rider who lacks confidence or a dog can smell fear.

In summary, our own trust in the goodness of life, and in the goodness of our children, is preeminent in any trying situation no matter what the seeming evidence to the contrary. Through our ongoing kindness in the midst of the most painful of crises, we literally "smile our children into being."

When Life Isn't Full Speed Ahead

Later in this book, I'll be drawing an insight from the book *The Little Prince,* which was penned over seventy years ago. However, there's a statement in this story that's relevant to what I was learning in my life during this period. The statement is to the effect that straight ahead, you can't go very far. When a chosen path suddenly dead-ends, or veers in a quite different direction, something important is occurring with regard to our development.

In 2012, my husband and I decided to retire from the foundation we had created and run in honor of our first daughter, Sydney, who died when she was only twenty-four days old. For a dozen years we had organized fundraisers and in various other ways supported kids living with heart defects. Once you begin running a nonprofit and that ball gets rolling, it's nearly impossible to take a break from it. However, it was becoming painfully obvious that, with our accelerating healing from this tragedy, our personal need to continue running the foundation was receding, so that it was becoming more of a burden than a joy.

That said, since it was our own creation, I had a hard time figuring out how to quit the foundation. I sat with this discomfort for about a year. My husband had previously been diagnosed with allergies and asthma, and his lungs have always been his weak spot. But in 2011 he was sick every two weeks for eight straight months, which is highly abnormal for an otherwise healthy person. When we investigated, we discovered he had two rare immune disorders, one called CVID where his T cells and B cells don't communicate properly with each other, the other called MGUS where he has an abnormally high level of a particular protein. The consequence was that his immune system was compromised, which is why he so easily became sick.

I once heard the phrase "the four pillars of health," though I don't remember where I heard it. The expression stuck in my head, and I decided to devise my own pillars of health, which consist of obtaining an appropriate amount of sleep, eating healthily, exercising, and minimizing stress. Guided by these, we set about overhauling our lifestyle (which, incidentally, was already fairly clean to begin with.) One feature of this overhaul was to add various supplements to my husband's daily routine, which helped tremendously. Still, it was clear that despite the improvements he was experiencing in how he was feeling, reducing stress was still paramount.

My intuition told me we needed to retire from the foundation, closing it down, since our involvement in its highly stressful activities wasn't a necessity for our lives but optional. To take this route was however the opposite of what I had long assumed would be our course, since Brady, my youngest, was going to be entering kindergarten in the fall of 2012 and I had imagined myself running the foundation more or less full-time from that point on.

With Brady starting school and the foundation closed, I found myself wondering what to do with my time. Simultaneously, working with a particular grandmother in my therapy job was causing me burnout. Her extremely low level of education, exceeding harsh and punitive parenting practices, and resistance to almost anything I said had resulted in two fruitless years during which I had tried and failed to get through to her on key issues involving the raising of her grandson. Though this was the only career I had ever known, I couldn't take it anymore. But were I to quit on top of the changes already happening in my life, what would I do? Where would I be if I was no longer a therapist working with parents and kids?

I felt like I had been knocked off my base. No longer inspired by the foundation or my work, all I could do was trust that my future path would be illuminated somehow, someway.

This all came at a time when my daughter Faith was dealing with some pretty severe anxiety that had seemingly popped up out of nowhere although, of course, it wasn't actually from nowhere. I've learned that guidance comes in all kinds of forms, and so I keep my eyes and ears open in all the situations in which I find myself. As it happened, while we were engaged in the intake at a psychologist's office, the therapist asked me what I did for a living. When I told her, she inquired, "Aren't you burned out? Wouldn't you feel better working with a different population who actually want help?"

It was as if I had been struck by lightning, as I instantly recognized that I didn't need to totally change careers, only to work with a different clientele. As a result of this revelation, I spent October of that year in an exhaustive online review of masters level and doctoral level programs that would enable me to add to my portfolio a degree to allow me to work as a licensed psychologist in private practice, with the ability to take insurance. But as I surveyed the degrees related to marriage and family counseling, nothing spoke to me. I knew my intuition would tingle when I hit on the path I was supposed to take, and it wasn't happening.

Again, let me emphasize that guidance comes at the most unexpected moments and in the least predictable ways. I think it's this way because it teaches us that there's no aspect of our world and our lives that isn't permeated with the divine source from which we have all sprung. So it was that, while browsing Facebook one day, a quotation caught my eye. Although I don't remember the quotation now, I recall visiting the page of the parent coach who uttered it, and there I found what it was I wanted to pursue as my career: parent coaching. But when I went to this individual's website, I could find no information on where he went to school.

It occurred to me that a year earlier, a friend of mine, Cathy Adams, had mentioned in her podcast that she was a parent coach. When I learned where she had been trained, I called the founder of the program, filled out the application, was interviewed by phone, and began my training in December of 2012. Looking back on it, though there were periods of uncertainty, of not knowing the way, I always had faith I would intuit which way to go when the time was right.

CHAPTER 9

A Halloween Lesson for Mom

IT WAS 5:00 P.M. on Halloween Night when I screamed, "I hate Halloween! I wish I could just cancel it and send you all to bed at 5:30." I hadn't screamed at my twelve-year-old son in such a way for several years.

As he tried to explain to me what he was doing, I suddenly realized I had misheard him and consequently misunderstood what he was trying to say. Now I felt like a jerk.

Noah had been attempting to tell me he was doing a job his dad had just given him, whereas I thought he was complaining and telling me he had done all his jobs and wasn't doing any more.

I felt awful and apologized in a soft voice. But as I tried to explain that it had been a stressful week, during which I had a lot on my mind, I found myself crying so hard that I couldn't get the words out.

That particular year, Halloween had fallen on a Friday, which happened to round out a hectic week for me. I had been engaged in some exciting work projects that demanded my attention and concentration. Alongside these projects, I had been helping two friends work through their divorce. On top of this, I had also learned that a family member had cancer. And if this wasn't enough, I was forced to deal with a couple of situations that had arisen at my children's schools. The whole week long, there had been no time for myself.

I have learned over the past few years how important it is to be kind to myself by allowing time for self-care. Part of caring for myself is that I try hard to fit in exercise whenever possible. I also like to take time to read books, walk our dog, and spend some quiet moments alone. As an introvert, I find this a necessary part of my routine, for it's how I recharge myself.

So when the week culminating in Halloween didn't allow me to carve out time for myself, I suddenly found myself off center. Already edgy, coupled with the realization that my children's plans for Halloween were quite nebulous and therefore constantly changing, I was primed to explode. All it took was a simple misunderstanding.

As I reflected on what had transpired, I realized how I had allowed myself to be pulled so deeply into all the details of the week that, when my son spoke to me, I reacted from a completely unconscious state. By "unconscious," I mean that I wasn't at all present to what he was actually saying.

There was a lesson for me in this. No matter how many things are on my plate, I must prioritize to ensure I fit in time for self-regeneration. Had it been a normal week, I'm quite sure I wouldn't have launched into my son the way I did.

I also know it's damaging to beat myself up over

lashing out. So I quickly forgave myself, apologized again to my son, and made sure I got back to "myself" in order to avoid doing this again.

As events would have it, the following week was also busy and yet everything was quite different. Because I carved out time to slow down when the pressure was on, I felt much less edgy and far more peaceful. When I renew and recharge myself, I'm a kinder, gentler person.

CHAPTER 10

Why It's Essential to Develop Your Capacity for Kindness

A COLLEAGUE AND I were talking about our careers as parent coaches—how much we love our work and are committed to helping moms and dads become the parents they wish to be.

During our discussion, I confided in my colleague, "I lost a childhood friend to breast cancer this week. She would have turned thirty-nine in eleven days. She had a loving husband and left behind two adorable children, a three-year-old son and a two-year-old daughter." It so happened that October, the month in which she died, was breast cancer awareness month.

During the days that followed the devastating news of my friend's death, I thought a lot about my own parenting. What if I was to suffer the same fate, dying at a tragically young age and leaving my children with no mother?

As I looked at photos of my friend with her family, it crushed me to see her children and know they not only wouldn't get to be raised by their mom, but because they were so young, they would have few, if any, memories of her.

I tend not to let many fears get past my "protective bubble," since I find most fears evoke needless anxiety. In fact, I've become practiced at not giving attention to fears when they arrive on my mental doorstep. But one fear that seemed to sometimes find a way past my defenses was the fear of dying young and leaving my children motherless. In part, this is because, when I was little, I remember worrying that my mom would die early and leave me. Of course, in my rational mind I realize that, while I have just as much chance of this happening to me as any other mother, it's an unhelpful and pointless worry.

"You know," I told my colleague, "the conclusion I've come to is that my kids would be okay. The reason is that I can honestly say I'm about 95% of the parent I hope to be. Not 100%, because I believe there's always room for improvement. But overall, I'm deeply satisfied with the relationships I've built with my children."

My point in sharing this is to inspire. You see, I wasn't always the kind and caring mother I had grown to be. On the contrary, the frustration surrounding the Halloween incident I shared with you was once quite normal for me. But as a result of the insights gleaned from several parents and authors I admire, along with the lessons I've learned from my work as a therapist and parent coach, coupled with the things my own children have taught me, I can honestly say that were I to die tomorrow, I know in my heart my kids would understand that their mom loved them unconditionally—that they were the most precious parts of my life.

My relationship with each of my children is real, not artificial. They see me as a genuine human being—a person who makes mistakes, yes, but who isn't afraid to own these mistakes. I know I've imparted the values I hold dear, so that my daughter and sons understand thoroughly what character traits it's important to embody as they journey through life.

To get to the place I was able to feel good about myself as a parent wasn't easy, especially at first. I struggled mightily when my children were young. Routinely sleep-deprived, frequently overwhelmed, and stressed more often than not, many of my days were just not that much fun. In fact, it seemed almost every other mother I met was "happier" than me.

"What am I doing wrong?" I used to ask myself, for it was one of the most challenging periods of my life, which is surely saying something considering my firstborn child had died in my arms as an infant.

To admit I found parenting little people more difficult than coping with the loss of a child tells you how immensely challenging it can be to be a new mother, the mother of a toddler, or a mother with children in their teens. Often with few periods of respite, raising children can be just plain demanding.

The challenge children bring to us can be allowed to stymie us, or it can give us a reason to rise to a new level of functioning. I chose the latter and, if you haven't already, you can too.

I have always said that I want to live my life with no regrets. Over time, there have been a few choices I've made that caused regret, but for the most part this mindset has served me well. Consequently, I determined to apply this to parenting, working tirelessly to be the best parent I could be. The book you are reading now contains the insights that in due course allowed my Halloween outburst at my son to become a rarity in our relationship.

My Insurance Policy

Our relationships with those who are dear to us are so complex, there's always room for misunderstanding. So, in case anything should ever happen to end our connection prematurely, over the years I've taken out an insurance policy to make sure my children know how much they meant to me, how deeply I loved them, and why I did some of the things I did.

This insurance policy is in the form of a notebook I've kept for each of my children since the day they were born––a notebook in which I write letters to them about things they did or said, along with how I felt about them on a particular day.

I initially began this practice so my children could read the letters years in the future and learn about events they were too young to remember. Later, I came to realize that these notebooks would in due course furnish them with handwritten evidence of just how much I loved them and how committed I have been to being their mom. To fulfill this role is the single most important honor in my life. Having these records comforts me with the knowledge that if some tragedy befalls me, my daughter Faith, and two sons Noah and Brady, will have this lasting gift from me. Knowing this helps usher out any fear that attempts to intrude on our relationship.

When I learned of my friend's death in the evening of the day it occurred, I didn't immediately tell my kids. The following morning, a school day, I awoke to find my nine-year-old daughter and seven-year-old son already dressed, having taken their vitamins and set out the breakfast items. They were both so eager to create this surprise for me, having no awareness of the sadness in their mama's heart. It was such a warm, loving, and comforting gesture from these two little people—just what I needed at such a time.

These "sunset moments," as Rachel Macy Stafford refers to them, are the sweetest. I find they carry me through the more difficult, challenging, sad times. It's important to slow down long enough to recognize beautiful moments like these when they occur, allowing ourselves the opportunity to fully appreciate them.

As for cancer, it sucks. I wish it never existed. I know there's nothing I can do about it, other than eat well, exercise, get adequate sleep, manage my stress levels, microwave food in something other than plastic, along with all the other practices that can tip the scales in our favor. But the fact is, cancer is sometimes just bad luck.

Since it isn't my mission in life to try to cure cancer, what can I do? I can and will live my life in honor of my friend Tori and all the beautiful souls who have lost their lives to breast cancer or any other form of cancer. They may no longer be on this earth, but I am; and as long as I am, I will continue to try to make this world a less toxic, healthier, and better place for all of us who are blessed enough to inhabit it.

There is something else I can do, even more important. As I talked with my colleague about Tori's death, she helped me articulate what had been in my heart for quite a while but had never been spelled out. Since I personally know how fulfilling it is to have a strong, healthy relationship with my children, I want to help other parents experience this. Sharing this desire with my colleague, it all came into focus for me that morning. My work as a PCI Certified Parent Coach® is the vehicle through which I'm called to serve during my time on earth—something I've long known deep down, but that I could now make explicit. Helping parents become more conscious in their relationships with their children is what I'm here to do.

Imagine a world in which all parents related to their children with kindness. Without the undertow of all the evils wrought by the disturbed individuals engendered by upbringings that are less than kind, our world would be so transformed, the possibilities for what we could accomplish as a species would be limitless.

A Eulogy for the Living

I began my 42nd birthday by waking up with the people I love the most in the world, sending them on their way for the day. Quite an ordinary thing to do on a Tuesday morning in September, but I can't think of a place I would rather have been.

At the gym that morning, I got my butt kicked in my favorite class. Still, it felt pretty good to be able to work out hard, even though I'm not quite up to what I was in my twenties. It inspires me to watch women in the class who are easily twenty years older than me, yet who work out just as hard, if not harder.

A large part of my day was spent in an equally ordinary manner, dealing with the flea problem our new kitten brought home from the shelter. With the help of some very effective medicine from the vet, we were getting the problem under control, which pleased me to no end. The reward for my efforts was to celebrate with my family that evening. Nothing equals having my loved ones all together.

If you've read Antoine de Saint-Exupery's classic *The Little Prince*, you'll know that the little fellow adored sunsets. On his journey through the universe, visiting seven planets in all, what most made him sad was to leave the fifth one he had landed on because "it was blessed with one thousand, four hundred forty sunsets every twenty-four hours." Well, like him, I am enormously fond of sunsets; in fact, they are among my favorite things in the entire world. So, as a birthday gift, my husband painted an absolutely beautiful sunset for me.

Along with my painting, he gave me a Tree of Life necklace, because I love all that a tree represents—strength, stability, the cycle of life, growth, rebirth.

My youngest made me a card and put one dollar of his very own money into it. I thought that was so sweet! A friend gave me two perfectly shaped wine glasses that I love, and my daughter made me a card she created with the input of my husband, kids, mother-in-law, niece, and nephew, inscribing words that highlight my qualities. It's one of the most touching gifts I've ever received. I love that she brought everyone together to create it, and the words they composed are so special.

I often think of the concept of a living eulogy, during

which we tell people what we appreciate about them now, rather than waiting to say it in a speech following their death. I try to do this as often as possible with as many people as I can, and my sweet girl did it for me on my birthday.

One thought occurs to me in all of this that transcends everything else. It's that occasions such as a death, a birthday, or other celebrations such as anniversaries reveal the kindness in our hearts toward one another. On these days, we dive beneath our troubles and disagreements, touching the bedrock of kindness that's basic to us all.

Isn't this the way we should be living each and every day?

CHAPTER 11

The Teen Years and the Fine Art of Negotiation

ALTHOUGH MY TWELVE-YEAR-OLD isn't quite a teen, for all intents and purposes he acts like one. This isn't all bad, by the way; I happen to very much enjoy teenagers.

The other morning, Noah said he was tired and didn't want to go to church. Since I've felt that way many times myself, I decided to let him lay low. On my way out the door, I reminded him, "Staying home to rest doesn't mean you have permission to play video games the entire time we're gone." Tiredness is one thing, a morning of endless video games quite another. I also asked him to do his laundry and clean his room while the rest of the family were out.

On the way home from church, we stopped at the park with my younger two. While we were there, Noah called to ask whether he could play video games now, since he was well rested. My first instinct was to say no, but I held my tongue and asked whether his room was clean and his laundry done. When he replied in the affirmative on both counts, I decided that since church was technically over and the other two were having fun, video games would be fine.

The washing machine was running when I arrived home

sometime later. But when I went upstairs, I discovered that his room hadn't been cleaned. Feeling frustrated, I called him upstairs. "Do you recall our conversation when you called me, during which you told me you had performed the chores I asked you to do?"

When he claimed he didn't realize I expected him to clean his room, I felt all the more frustrated, at this point raising my voice until, not long into my ranting, he pointed out, "You're still yelling, even though I'm already cleaning my room." He was and I was. I shut my mouth and took a deep breath.

Going inside myself, sitting in silence while Noah simply looked at me, I realized that ranting was creating the very distance between us that I was trying to close. When I at last spoke, I was much calmer. "I don't know whether you heard me when I asked about your room," I said. "Only you know the truth. But I do know you distinctly said it was done."

I told him that, instead of half-listening, I try to give him my undivided attention when he talks to me, since this is one way I honor him as my son. "Because I'm fully present when I say something, I know what was said," I explained, "though I'm not at all sure you gave me the same consideration when we spoke on the phone."

I described how, because I felt he had dishonored my request, it seemed to me he was disrespecting me. I then explained, "During the next eight years, my goal is to raise you to be a competent, successful, independent adult. As far as your room goes, when the time comes that you live alone, you can keep your stuff any way you wish. But when you are in college and have a roommate, or if you choose to marry, you're going to have to be willing to live in a civilized way other people can tolerate. It's my job to prepare you for this, which is why I insist you keep your room tidy and put your laundry away as soon as it's done."

As we discussed what awaited us during the adolescent years, I pointed out there would be things I was willing to give in on, even though I might feel differently about them, whereas there would be other matters on which I was unwilling to bend. "That's just the way it is," I said.

We went on to talk about how, in order to get through the adolescent years not only loving each other but liking each other, we were both going to have to compromise probably a lot. I pointed out that it had been a compromise on my part to allow him to play video games after he called me. The truth was, I didn't really want him playing video games but felt it was fair since he claimed to have done what I asked of him.

During our conversation, Noah was much quieter and, rather than arguing, paid close attention to what I was saying. We ended the conversation understanding each other, feeling closer to each other, and with a clean room. Most importantly, we achieved this without any form of punishment.

A Better Way than Compromise

When I was originally composing this chapter, I planned to present five reasons adolescence should be renamed "the fine art of compromise." However, the term compromise is susceptible to different meanings.

The dictionary describes compromise as a middle state between conflicting opinions, reached by mutual concession or modification. There's a potential problem with this, illustrated by a quip someone once made that if you want beef but not potatoes, and I want potatoes but not beef, if we compromise and meet in the middle, we end up with a hash and then neither of us is happy.

Another dictionary definition of compromise is that it involves an agreement or settlement of a dispute reached "by each side making concessions." This is why we often hear that the secret to a happy marriage is to compromise a lot. People give up something in order to keep the other happy. But what if they are being asked to give up something that's really important to them, while the other party sees their willingness to give it up as equally important?

If you think about the idea of making concessions, it's not a big step before a concession becomes a way of selling ourselves out. We cave under pressure, accepting something we really don't agree with. This is one of the ways in which so many people in romantic relationships in my experience, especially women end up saying, "I completely lost myself in my relationship, to the point I no longer knew who I was."

As relationships develop, no matter what kind of relationship, what tends to happen is that the relationship becomes so important to us that we don't like to rock the boat and risk losing it. There's enough stress in life, and we certainly don't need the added stress of locking horns with someone with whom we live or work. So we get in the habit of giving up things that are important to us. Basically, we sell ourselves out to keep some semblance of peace.

The spiritual teacher Adyashanti shared an insight regarding compromise and how to tell when we are indulging in it. He writes, "When the person panics, goes for the quick solution, then it's always compromise." He adds, "Be patient with life, trust. There is space in not knowing, in not deciding." Finally, he reminds us, "In wise living, you are in synchronicity. You do not strategize your existence. You are in flow."

Compromise has been the way many of us have conducted our affairs for a very long time, but it's fundamentally different from living life in flow. Thankfully, today more and more of us are becoming aware of the importance of being true to ourselves by flowing with the essence of our being. We're learning that, if we wish to experience a fulfilling life, we have to become a person who honors what matters to us "come hell or high water." This is true in a marriage, and it's also true for parents and their growing offspring. We all have to develop the skills to work with another person without compromising *ourselves*.

For this reason, I prefer to use a different word from compromise. I like the word "negotiate." Negotiation promotes a spirit of cooperation between parent and child.

I hear many parents lament what they refer to often with an exasperated sigh as "the teen years." But there's no reason a child's teenage years have to be a combative struggle of "us against them." When we are willing to negotiate with our children, we feel more connected to them, and them to us. Maintaining a loving connection is a wonderful way to help our children move toward adulthood.

Negotiation models for our kids how to get along with others. No one would ever advise a colleague that the best way to get what they want in the workplace is to rant and rave, insisting things get done the way they want them done. Nor would we do this with our friends. So why do we get caught in the trap of thinking this is an effective way to deal with our kids? All it does is breed resentment, which leads to resistance and, if sustained, eventually outright rebellion as the child becomes old enough to tell us to take a flying leap.

When our kids were toddlers and preschoolers, we could perhaps teach them how to do something and insist they do it our way although many of us can vouch for the fact this method doesn't even work with young kids much of the time! However, when our children are approaching adolescence, these are years when they are seriously training to become adults. It's our responsibility as parents to grant them the increasing freedom to make their own choices. Teaching them the art of negotiating is a way to help them find their feet in their relationships, and as such is a vital aspect of preparing them for adulthood.

A caveat about our children's choices: when they get it wrong, it isn't our place to deliver an "I told you so" speech. Instead, we stand with them, empathize with how it feels to make a mistake, then support them in figuring out how to address the error—a topic we discussed in an earlier chapter.

When we compromise on things, we can easily end up settling for the lowest common denominator. Negotiation is fundamentally different, in that, instead of trying to hold onto ground, it involves finding ways to break new ground. Rather than trying to give away as little as we can, we seek to maximize the benefits for all parties. It's not about losing as little as we have to, and resenting what we had to let go of, but about creating win-win solutions everyone can be happy with.

When we practice the art of negotiation, our children see us as someone who is in their corner, standing with them, instead of against them. In contrast, compromise has a wholly different feel. Instead of coming from strength, it's about exploiting each other's weaknesses. None of us enjoy having to surrender things that matter to us, and when we feel forced to do so, a relationship becomes a dance in which we're always being careful not to step on the other's toes too much. That's no way to have fun together.

I constantly see adolescents who truly believe their parents try to make their life miserable. Compromise can be a way of reducing the degree of resentment, but it's still playing on a losing team, which will always result in varying degrees of misery.

In contrast, I also know teens who don't believe their parents are trying to make their life miserable, but who understand that mom and dad are on their team. Indeed, the most important predictor of the long-term health of our relationship with our children is that they know in their heart we are standing beside them, in their corner, as they emerge into adulthood.

How to Negotiate with Your Kids

Maximizing the enjoyment in a relationship means holding out for what really matters to us. Learning to stand our ground is therefore crucial.

To illustrate, I don't allow phones in the bedroom at night—a stand that isn't up for negotiation. Even though my twelve-year-old doesn't like my position on this, he knows from so many other things in our life together that I always have his best interests at heart. Consequently, he honors my wish on this. I'm well aware, however, that as the years go by, the time will come when we will need to renegotiate this issue.

Whenever we take a stand, it's important to ask ourselves whether we are really being true to ourselves or just insisting on getting our way. Resistance, insistence, and defiance can feel like we're defining ourselves, when actually they are counterfeits. The "feel" is entirely different from that of self-definition. Resistance, insistence, and defiance carry an emotional charge that to be true to ourselves doesn't require, for there's simply a quiet firmness.

Truly being ourselves means we are neither compliant, defiant, nor even resistant. Instead, we are open to consider the other person's insights. Then, we determine whether incorporating them into our life would be selling ourselves out, or whether it might be a new aspect of being true to ourselves because it's in line with where we want things in general to go.

For matters that require a joint decision, it's important to recognize no one gets everything they want all the time.

Instead of settling for peace at any price by compromising, it's helpful if we each come from a position of strength and thereby expand the boundaries of the relationship we enjoy as parent and child. The aim is to open up new frontiers of fulfillment. Exploring new avenues together, instead of arguing about who gets to win, we blaze the trail to a more satisfying life than either of us has experienced before.

To arrive at solutions, we must know what's truly important to us. Knowing ourselves enables us to distinguish what we absolutely have to have from what can be surrendered without any loss of our personhood. If we don't know ourselves well enough to recognize what's essential, we add insecurity to our uncertainty and tend to cling to a lot of things that for a secure and self-aware person would be negotiable. The more we are in touch with our deepest feelings instead of just our surface emotions and whims, the better our ability to negotiate based on what really counts.

During a negotiation, we have to hold onto ourselves and not take the other person's wishes personally. How can the person honestly put their cards on the table if we are going to take what they have to say personally? Nothing—absolutely nothing—is worth taking personally. Practical problems require practical solutions. We need to treat them in a matter-of-fact manner.

People who have a weak sense of themselves don't hold onto themselves long enough to find creative solutions. Feeling threatened, they become defensive. Then, instead of negotiating, it becomes a battle in which "winner takes all."

When we are solidly grounded in our essence, we don't

need to take a defensive "I gotta be me" approach, which is basically telling the other to take a hike. Thus, we're on the path to an effective negotiation when we can allow another person's insights to have an impact on us. Holding onto ourselves allows us to take the other's best interests into consideration without feeling we are losing ourselves.

To value what a person wants doesn't imply we have to change what *we* want, or that the other should change what they want. There's nothing more futile than trying to get a person to change. On the other hand, to value the other *does* mean accepting that the person has valid reasons for wanting to do things differently from us. It's possible to disagree without being disagreeable. Accepting differences gracefully enables us to experience the best that each of us has to bring to parenting, a relationship, a workplace, a friendship.

In any negotiation, the trick is to really listen to what the other believes to be essential. This involves recognizing that our wishes and those of the other hold equal weight. It requires paying attention to our tendency to put down the other's desires. Even if we think the person's wishes are foolish, they're valid in that person's eyes, and achieving solutions requires treating them as such. Without giving up our essential self, we seek to appreciate an issue from the other's point of view, looking for a way forward that respects the concerns of both parties. No longer needing to annihilate the other's separate reality, we search for a win-win solution.

The goal is to satisfy the maximum number of concerns of both parties without selling ourselves out. And if one of us has to choose to go along with the other because there has to be agreement and we can't find a way to incorporate the wishes of both—such as on what part of the country we are going to live in, or which school the children will go to—we can do so joyfully and not with resentment because it isn't our essential self that we're sacrificing. It's a *choice* we're making freely. Each time we incorporate into our life what's good of the other's perceptions, we aren't diminished but become *more* than we've so far known ourselves to be.

An Untidy Room

I was coaching a mom who was exceedingly frustrated by her son's messy room. Explaining that she is a very neat person and has taught her son to be neat, she said it felt to her as if he wasn't respecting either his things or her, since he allowed his room to stay messy. This mom has an otherwise wonderful, connected relationship to her son.

While we were on the phone one day, the mother walked up into her son's room to describe to me just what she saw. She noticed an old wristband on the floor from when they went on a family getaway weekend. She saw a truck that her own mother had given to her son. Then her eyes fell upon a certificate that he received at school. At this point, she unexpectedly became excited and started speaking rapidly and with enthusiasm as the reality of the situation began to dawn on her. "I can hardly believe it," she told me. "I'm suddenly seeing my son's room through new lenses, I am seeing his room as *he* sees his room."

We're talking about a sweet, caring, sensitive boy.

Objects that are special to him are those that have emotional value for him. The family lives a rather minimalist lifestyle, and the mother now realized that all of the items she had been seeing as junk on his bedroom floor were actually his precious trinkets, items that recall for him a warm memory of a loved one. She also realized he had no means of storing these mementos, which was why they were on the floor.

When the boy arrived home from school that day, his mother told him of her realization and her idea to get him a means of storing his things. He was very excited about their plan, and the next weekend they bought and installed storage bins, shelves, and a cork board. Now, all of his special things have a home of their own and he has no trouble at all keeping his room tidy.

By understanding what was important to her son, this mom was able not only to forge a deeper connection with him, but was also able to creatively figure out a way where both she and her son could be happy with the outcome of the situation.

Tackle Your Own Issues in Order to Be True to Yourself

When we see someone tackle their own issues instead of either picking fights or selling out, we can't help but develop a respect for the person. The relationship moves out of a destructive mode, in which each tries to get the better of the other or merely puts up with the other, into one that capitalizes on each person's strengths.

Love thrives in an atmosphere of respect for a person's strength, measured by their ability to be true to themselves while remaining deeply connected to the other. Taking the path of least resistance, which compromise so often involves, weakens love because it leads to a stalemate (pun intended) in which the parties eventually resent each other. Mediocrity becomes the order of the day and our enthusiasm for each other wanes. Years later, we wonder how we lost the connection we once enjoyed.

It isn't easy for a parent to practice the art of negotiation, since it means our children are going to increasingly feel their power as they become individuals who can be true to themselves at all times. However, the aim of being able to say what matters to them isn't so they can live a life in which they are disconnected from us, holding us at arm's length. The point is for parent and child to at last be able to come close to each other as strong adults, with neither party losing themselves. This is where fulfillment lies. This is the goal of effective parenting.

While driving in the car with me recently, my nine-year-old daughter told me casually what makes a good friend. These were her words: "All it takes to be a good friend is kindness, generosity, and sweetness from the heart." This same child made up a club with her friends, and here are the rules for their club:

1.   No fighting
2.   Everyone is allowed to join
3.   Listen to everyone's ideas
4.   Be fair
5.   Be honest

Not a bad summation of what's required for a successful negotiation. In fact, we could take this recipe for how to be a good friend, along with Faith's rules of her club, and apply them to almost any situation we can think of in the world. Doesn't this seem like a recipe for successful interactions among human beings, whether in our personal relationships, our communities, our places of work, or as nations sharing a world?

Imagine for a moment what the world would look like if everyone lived by this little girl's wisdom.

CHAPTER 12

Learning to Work Together

MY SEVEN-YEAR-OLD son has always been, let's say, creative and smart. This has played out over his lifetime thus far in the form of being both determined and sneaky!

Like many kids today, including his older brother Noah, Brady loves video games. I have tried over the years to place limits on his usage, but he manages to find a way around my rules and limits, which ends up with repercussions for him.

A year or two ago, I got fed up with the way all three of my kids were obsessed with handheld devices, so I purchased a lockbox to store them in. Since I controlled the access, they were allowed screen time only when I deemed it appropriate. This worked fairly well, in that it brought the use of the devices under control.

But there's a caveat.

The repercussions of Brady's sneakiness with respect to his DS meant it stayed in the lockbox for such long periods that he pretty much forgot about it. However, when he had to spend a whole week home from school because he was sick, I took pity on the fact he was unwell and dug the DS out of the box for him to play with.

After such a long time without the DS, and no mention of it, I had imagined the excessive time he used to spend with it was no longer an issue. Except that, the moment it was out of the box, he was asking for it whenever he had two minutes of downtime!

It suddenly dawned on me that the only reason my strategy of locking the video games away had worked was because the children didn't have access to the devices, *not* because they were learning how to make smart choices for themselves in terms of how they use technology.

After talking with a good friend, I came to some important realizations. I have always tried to live my life from a mindset of abundance. This frame of mind normally allows me to have a positive outlook on most things in life. Now I saw how negative my decision to lock the video devices away was. Not only that, but preventing my kids from having access to their cherished games was actually teaching them to live their lives from a place of scarcity. This was opposite of how I want them to live.

When I went through my own parent coaching two years prior to this, I came to the realization that one of my most important goals as a parent is to raise my children to be independent adults. The coaching work I engaged in brought home to me the fact that, from the time our children are born, they are moving toward adulthood every step of the way. It's a process that's irreversible, irrevocable, and therefore needs not opposition on our part as parents, but our encouragement and support. Consequently, I resolved that all of my decisions in the realm of parenting needed to be in alignment with this goal.

It was plain to me now that locking the video devices in

a box and only allowing access to them when I deigned to grant access was doing nothing toward moving my children closer to becoming independent adults.

It was time for a conversation with Brady. "I've noticed how much you are growing up," I began, "and consequently I've been wondering whether you might be ready to handle a little more responsibility along with increased freedom." He was very curious what I was referring to. "I think we might have a go at no longer locking the DS in the lockbox," I suggested. "But only if you think you're truly ready for that."

Brady's response was decidedly enthusiastic, declaring he was definitely ready. So we talked about how, were we to leave his DS in his drawer for instance, he might handle it in a mature, responsible manner. "It's not okay for you to sneak it out when you aren't supposed to," I explained. "You have to make wise choices."

This led us into a great conversation about how to live a healthy life and what that looks like. I explained that, each day before screens, he needed to do his homework and chores (assuming he had such that particular day.) He needed to play outside, get together with friends, or do something else that was fun but didn't involve screens. He needed to make healthy eating choices. He also needed to engage in some reading. "If you do all those things every day, you'll be living a very good, healthy life," I explained. In line with my parenting goals, he would also be moving closer to learning how to be a successful, independent adult.

Brady was ready to accept the challenge.

We started the new approach at the beginning of the

next school week, when he was well enough to return to class. The DS remained in his drawer, and he proved himself to be amazingly responsible and ethical. The first week, following school, he and his friend spent most of their afternoons trying, in their little seven-year-old way, to figure out how to structure their time together to get their homework done and play outside, while still squeezing in some DS time at the end of it all.

What most impressed me was the way that, each day during these planning sessions (they had no idea I was listening), Brady continued to focus on not even trying to get the DS out until he could say he had engaged in all the requirements. I also loved the way his friend supported him in this mission.

As the week progressed, several times I pointed out what good choices my son was making and how proud I was of him. I told him he was certainly right when he said he was ready for the increased responsibility. It was a fabulous week, such a change from our earlier struggles over the amount of time spent on video devices or being the mean mom who finally, in exasperation, locked them away!

Why did this plan not only work well but also feel good? When I reflected on Brady's response to the challenge with which I presented him, I realized this approach was successful because it was in complete alignment with my values in terms of a life that consisted of more than screen time, while also fulfilling my goal of preparing my kids for independence and living from a mindset of abundance.

In contrast, I now saw I had locked up the devices out of frustration and fear. The truth is, I was terrified all three of them would become screen junkies! Talking it through with my friend and realigning my actions with my goal helped move us in a positive, productive direction.

Not only that, but giving Brady additional freedom, supported by my watchful eye and encouragement, has resulted in him experiencing success with being responsible. This in turn afforded us lots of opportunities to bond over his great choices. As I observed him feeling increasingly confident about himself, I in turn enjoyed feeling proud of my boy.

We come back to an insight we've encountered several times, which is that it's feeling bad about themselves that causes children to act out, whereas good behavior is tied to feeling valued, valuable, and therefore confident.

Given what I've learned about parenting, it's not surprising how a simple shift in perspective can result in such a dramatic change for the better in a child's behavior. Nevertheless, it continues to amaze me every time I see it happen, both with my clients and in my own life. In Brady's case, all it took to bring about a change was a shift on my part from fear to kindness.

We are the best parents we can be when we are in alignment with our values, while at the same time seeing our children for the amazing little beings they are, then taking those trusting steps that in an age-appropriate way draws this out of them.

CHAPTER 13

To Instill Fear in a Child Is a Disastrous Parenting Technique

I OFTEN HEAR people say, "I wouldn't want to bring a child into today's world." For some, it can even be a moral issue, especially given the threat of terrorism, the possibility of a nuclear nightmare, and the squalor and poverty that results from overpopulation of the planet, let alone the environmental damage. They ask, "Is it right to bring a child into a world where there's so much suffering?"

The human species certainly endures an Everest of suffering, and technology has made it possible to wreak havoc on human beings on a scale unparalleled in history. Hiroshima and Nagasaki bear witness to the modern potential for mass destruction. Armies have sailed and marched ever since the dawn of the agricultural revolution, when humans first began putting down roots, establishing communities that could be plundered and therefore needed defending. But nothing on the scale of the 20th century had ever occurred, an era when we slaughtered in excess of 100 million of our own species.

In his stunning critique of our society, Ernest Becker in

his classic Pulitzer Prize Winner *The Denial of Death* describes an earthquake burying 70,000 alive in Peru, while a tidal wave washes more than a quarter of a million into the Indian Ocean all of this quite apart from what humans do to one another. Says Becker, "Creation is a nightmare spectacular taking place on a planet that has been soaked for hundreds of millions of years in the blood of all creatures." As Becker points out, these are facts we like to forget, since it takes what he refers to as "heroic dedication" to risk living with such awareness.

In generations past, young men were conscripted into armies that marched across continents plundering and destroying, with their families back home not knowing whether they were alive or had perished as the years of their absence went by. One of the differences today is that we receive news from every corner of the planet all but instantaneously. Consequently, as one observer points out, we know that four little Palestinian boys playing soccer on a beach in Gaza, all from the same family, were killed by a missile, while the next day a missile took a plane full of people down to their death as it approached an airport in the Ukraine.

On one level, anyone who is at all in touch with the state of the world can't help but fear for their children's future. Just read the newspaper or turn on the television news, and you'll quickly find plenty in the world to stoke your fears.

However, beginning with 9/11, my sense is that we took a step toward becoming a *culture* of fear, which is an experience of fear at a whole new level—despite the fact that fear is the last emotion we need to parent effectively.

How 9/11 Affected My Desire to Bring a Child into the World

I suspect my experience of 9/11 was quite different from that of most others. I remember it vividly where I was when I first heard the shocking news on the radio, seeing the images of the plane hitting the first tower, followed by the second, on television later in the day, then both towers collapsing in a dizzying, surreal few moments. I remember feeling that, in that instant, the world might very well be going to hell in a hand basket. It was a confusing and scary time for everyone.

But unlike most on that day, my world had been turned upside down and my life turned inside out five months and ten days before the events of 9/11. You see, my firstborn daughter, Sydney, had died in my arms of a heart defect. As a bereaved parent, I had spent since April 1st of that year trying to figure out how to get myself back on my feet again emotionally, mentally, spiritually, energetically, and physically.

We wanted to have another child. So by 9/11, my husband Jay and I were already in the midst of fertility treatments trying to have a baby (who would become our much-loved twelve-year-old son.) Terrible as 9/11 was, together with the culture of fear it spawned, my focus was more on what I was undergoing as I sought to rebuild my hopes of being a mother.

I recall standing in a stream of water in the shower the night of 9/11, my emotions churning, my thoughts racing. The thought that was predominant after the jarring events of the day may shock you. In a strange way, I felt a measure of relief. Somehow, the fact that the country, even much of the world, was united in a shared grief that day was comforting to me. It was as if I was no longer suffering alone, but we were all participating in the common suffering of our species. Finally, people who met me and spoke with me might glean some inkling of the pain, the grief, the sorrow I had been living with for months now. As a result of 9/11, I no longer felt like an alien in a strange land.

Another dominant thought that evening as I stood there in the shower was that the fact my child was dead meant I at least didn't have to fear for her safety at such a scary time. Oddly, that realization brought me a small measure of comfort too. I thought of all the parents who must be in agony as they awaited news of whether their loved ones had survived the attacks.

It wasn't long before a further thought occurred to me: "Am I nuts? Do I really want to bring another child into this crazy, mixed-up, scary, violent world?"

My immediate answer was a resounding "Yes!" As far back as I can remember, I had dedicated my life to trying to make the world a better place. Now, the realization dawned on me that having more children wasn't just a matter of building our own family; it was that Jay and I needed to bring children into the world because the world needed these children we would give birth to and raise. It was our responsibility in life to work tirelessly to nurture kids who would not only be good citizens, decent human beings, but who at heart would be kind and therefore in turn join us in the task of making the world a better place.

Sailing Upstream with Kindness

I'm sure you've been in an office sometime, or a room in someone's home, that's equipped with one of those surveillance cameras that constantly click away. After a while, you don't notice the clicking, or even the unceasing movement, of these surveillance devices, and yet it never stops. That's the way the anxiety triggered by 9/11 functions. As a culture, we are never wholly free of it, so that it causes us to be on constant alert, wearing us down.

We certainly don't need more unconscious people in the world, the kind who fly planes into buildings, who wreak havoc throughout Africa in the form of the Islamist militants Boko Haram, or who butcher innocent people in the nightmare that's the Islamic State. On the other hand, the need for children who grow up differently, true to their naturally kind self, is greater than ever.

Fourteen years after 9/11, I am deeply grateful for my wonderful family, which has caused me to renew my commitment to my kids and to our shared future. In honor of all those souls who lost their lives in the tragic events of 9/11, I will continue to work hard to do my part to make the world a kinder, more caring place, with my offspring by my side bringing comfort to people who are suffering, reaching out to help individuals in need, spreading cheer and goodwill wherever they go, and following their heart's whispers so they use their talents to leave a kindly mark on the planet.

You can see, then, that my family and I are sailing upstream when it comes to the culture of fear so many of us have been immersed in since 9/11. Whereas so many in our society live with a backdrop of fear underlining everything they do, we are determined not to succumb to this paranoia. To counteract it, I take time each evening to truly be with our children. I look at each of them, seeing them for the amazing young people they are. I tell them what's in my heart. I find that when the sharing is open and honest, a child's trust flourishes, and with it the kindness with which they venture into the world to make a difference.

When, as a family, we are outside the home, we make it a point to tell a coworker or friend how much we appreciate them. We rebuild a burned bridge when it's needed. We reach out a hand to someone who could use it. Big or small, every act of kindness we send out into the world helps calm the pervasive fear engendered by 9/11, little by little quelling the culture of fear that was born that day.

CHAPTER 14

Kindness in the Classroom

ONE OF THE PRIMARY venues in which kindness can have a huge impact is our children's classrooms. However, sadly, the classroom has often been an outlet for brutal treatment of children, and at times outright sadism. Thankfully, a more humane atmosphere prevails in many classrooms today—something we should celebrate and encourage.

If your children have kind teachers, unlike many teachers years ago, do you ever stop to share your gratitude for the wonderful influence they have on your kids day in and day out?

I think particularly of one of my daughter's teachers, Mrs. Asaro, and her school's principal, Mrs. Hofstrom. In our town, students move to a new school when going into second grade, fourth grade, and sixth grade. When it came my daughter's turn to change schools for fourth grade, I expected it to be a bit rough for her, since she's sensitive, becomes attached to her teachers and the staff, and takes time to adjust to new people in a new environment. She works hard to form relationships.

Sunday evening before the fourth day of school, at

bedtime, Faith began complaining that she had a stomachache. Whenever she's stressed, worried, or scared about something, her stomach is the first thing to alert us to the fact. When I reminded her of this, she thought for a moment, but concluded that she wasn't aware of anything bothering her.

Monday morning, she continued to complain about her stomach, although she still went off to school. That afternoon, when classes were out, she was fine. But when it was time to go to bed, as she was getting her things ready for the next day, her stomach started hurting again. By morning, she was in so much discomfort that she didn't want to go to school at all. Since by now she was clearly late, I sat down with her and helped her examine, then articulate, what was bothering her. Once she started talking, the floodgates opened.

"I hate school," she declared.

Hmm, I thought to myself. *I wonder what's going on, because this is a child who loves school.*

Despite the fact that the dire future she had begun imagining for herself could only ever result from taking a path she would never go down, since it isn't in her to behave in such a manner, she had convinced herself that because of the stricter discipline policy at this school, she was going to earn demerits, which would lead to her being suspended, following which she would be expelled.

What were the stricter rules? For a start, she wasn't allowed to throw away her trash at lunchtime until the end of lunch—a practice quite different from her previous school. Plus, the very first job she had been assigned to perform on behalf of the class was to be the line leader—a responsibility that caused her to feel worried sick lest she lead the students the wrong way when they had to move to the next class. To cap things off, she didn't get to see her two best friends in school—something I could do little about, other than to schedule play dates on the weekends, which I made sure happened.

After listening closely to her list of woes, I thanked her for being so open and honest. "There's nothing we can't talk about," I reassured her. "There's no problem I won't help you with." Her face reflected measured relief.

The next task was to address each concern in turn. By the time we had talked through all of them, she felt much better and her stomachache had subsided. Despite how late she was for school, she declared herself ready to go.

When we arrived at the school, I asked whether her teacher was free so we could let her know what was going on. Unfortunately, she wasn't; and as we sat in the school office, Faith became quite sad. At that moment, the new principal noticed us as she was heading out the door. Pausing to ask my daughter what was wrong, she commented reassuringly, "I don't like to see students feeling sad."

"Do you have a few minutes for us to talk to you," I inquired.

"Well, I'm on my way to a meeting," the principal said with a sigh. Then, realizing her assistance was truly required, she turned to the office manager and instructed, "Let them know I'll be late." Turning back to us, she invited us into her office.

After I briefly highlighted what was bothering Faith, Mrs. Hofstrom calmly, and in a soothing voice, reiterated all I had shared with Faith before we had left home. Then, when I explained that Faith was the Line Leader this week and was nervous she might lead the class the wrong way, Mrs. Hofstrom lowered her voice, leaned over, looked Faith in the eye, and reminded my daughter that this was her own first year at the school also, which meant she didn't know all the protocols either. Consequently, she herself needed to ask numerous questions during the course of a day. In fact, some days when she came to school, she too felt downright scared.

At this, Faith's face lit up with relief. Her smile told me that she felt heard, understood, and connected. I said a quiet prayer of thanks for this angel arriving just when we needed her. Although we took up only about five minutes of her time, it was about the most powerful five minutes she could have given to my daughter. As we rose to leave her office, she assured Faith she would look for her later in the day and check in with her to make sure she was feeling okay.

A principal like this is proof to me that the schoolhouse, so often in bygone days the occasion for terror in the lives of countless children, has the potential in our more enlightened era to become a powerhouse of kindness. Whether it does depends in large measure on how we as parents value school personnel, relating to them with kindness and gratitude. It's we who must set the tone and create an atmosphere in the community that honors teachers and other school staff, thereby drawing out the best in them.

As I kissed Faith goodbye and watched her happily bounce down the hallway, my heartfelt a depth of gratitude and relief I can scarcely describe. Later that day when she came home, she was happy and reported that her principal had in fact found her and checked in on her. I had also emailed her teacher, who similarly pulled her aside to reassure her just the way Mrs. Hofstrom and I had done earlier. It often takes only a few moments to connect, and yet connection from a kind heart makes all the difference to the quality of a child's day, not to mention the entire "feel" of the educational system.

During that evening, there were no complaints of a stomachache, and none in the morning either. On the contrary, Faith's stomach felt completely fine and she was looking forward to going to school. The problem of a little girl's anxiety had been solved simply because, each and every day, there are kind, intelligent, dedicated individuals who devote their lives to teaching and guiding our children.

It's so easy to become caught up in the negative aspects of school, such as too much homework, too little movement, or too many standardized tests. In contrast, how wonderful it is to appreciate the increasing number of kind souls who spend their working life in the service of our young people.

Going the Extra Mile

It used to be that warnings of what it meant to become a "failure" were used both in homes and classrooms to try to motivate students to buckle down and learn their lessons. Punishments ranging from being made to stand in the corner, sent to the principal's office, awarded a detention, or being physically caned or spanked were meted out daily in an attempt to get children to learn.

Fear of failure turned out to be a poor motivator. For some time now, teachers everywhere have increasingly been discovering how kindness, enthusiasm, creativity, and caring are so much more successful in motivating students, since they build on and encourage the natural desire of children to be inquisitive and productive.

I have witnessed how, instead of shouting at kids and laying major emphasis on discipline, teachers who *connect* rather than correct all the time can make a huge difference in a child's education. Whereas fear causes children to draw back, shutting down, connecting with a child opens them up.

When my son was six, I accompanied him on a school field trip to a museum. A new student had joined the class a few months earlier, a little girl who had just moved from China and didn't speak a word of English. I can't begin to imagine how challenging this was for both the pupil and her teacher. But instead of seeing the lack of an ability to speak English as a nuisance, my son's teacher used it as an opportunity to connect.

While we were listening to a presentation about animal habitats in a classroom at the museum, Mrs. Winkler got down on the floor and crawled to where she could sit down next to the little girl from China. It turned out she had an app on her phone that allowed her to type English words into it and get a translation. This enabled the little girl to follow along whenever she didn't understand something that was being said. My son's teacher remained on the floor with the girl the entire time, continually typing into her phone the information the instructor was imparting to the kids about animal habitats. Now that's kindness.

It was so heartwarming to watch the little girl's face light up as the Chinese translation kept popping up on the screen and she was able to understand what the other kids were learning. I'm sure this youngster had no idea how fortunate she was to have landed in this wonderful teacher's classroom to commence her education in an English-speaking setting. The effort this teacher was putting forth was going to be immeasurably helpful to the girl. This teacher's creativity in using technology in this way, coupled with her boundless energy and dedication to her students, will have ripple effects into the future that are unfathomable. This, of course, is what Rachel Joy Scott's notion of a widening ripple of kindness is all about.

This wasn't the only outstanding act of kindness I witnessed during that field trip. Another teacher, Dr. Mueller, who happened to be a former teacher of my two other children, was sitting with a group of first graders from her classroom. Spread out on the floor and a bench in a hallway of the museum, they were intently writing on little strips of paper. Math is this teacher's first love, and seeking to inspire her students she had found a way to incorporate a math learning activity into a short downtime during their visit to the museum.

When I walked by this group several minutes later, their strips of paper bore the letters of the alphabet down the left side and they were trying to come up with objects they saw in the museum whose names began with each letter of the alphabet. This is the kind of interactive learning that builds children's enthusiasm instead of dampening it. Under the tutelage of such caring teachers, children retain the passion for learning with which they come into the world instead of being shut down by busywork.

Having had two children in this teacher's classroom two different years, I know how creative and passionate she is about her profession. She has an amazing ability to intuit the level of learning of each of her students, which enables her to find ways to encourage the kids who are functioning at a lower level, while also cheering on those who have the ability to race ahead. Her seemingly endless energy, caring, and kindness pour into the students in her classroom.

The ripple effect of the time investment, commitment, encouragement, and inspiration of such teachers is truly immeasurable as, following their heart's calling, they nurture our children's love of learning and thereby prepare the business people, inventors, office workers, scientists, health care workers, restaurateurs, mechanics, and leaders of tomorrow.

CHAPTER 15

How to Help Children Conquer Their Fears

MY OLDER SON decided he was ready to learn to ride a
bicycle just before his fourth birthday. After only three
days of working at it, he was riding. On the other hand, my
daughter took three summers to reach the point she could
ride her bike completely without training wheels.

Now it was the turn of my seven-year-old to show he
could ride without needing training wheels. Following in
the steps of his sister, his trainers had been "off and on" for
the past four summers. However, in his case there was an
added challenge. Whereas his sister seemed oblivious to the
boo-boos she could acquire by falling off, he was all too
aware of the dangers, which resulted in what I referred to as
a bit of "gravitational insecurity." It was this extreme
caution that had prevented him from just hopping on and
figuring it out as his older brother had done.

Brady had actually achieved the balance required to
ride a bicycle during the previous summer, so that only his
fear of falling and hurting himself kept him from taking off
without me holding the back of his bike. This summer, I
really wanted to see him ride on his own, especially since
the weekend of our annual thirty-seven person camping trip

(real camping, replete with tents) was imminent, when all the kids bring their bikes to ride around the campsite. Each year until now, Brady had brought only his scooter, which made it difficult for him to keep up with the other kids, most of whom were older.

"Wouldn't it be nice if you could learn how to ride before we leave for the trip, so you can ride with the other kids?" Given the way Brady went ballistic at this suggestion, I took it that my idea wasn't such a good one. The pressure of having to master the bike with a deadline looming was evidently more than he could bear. He was so upset, he gritted his teeth, as his face turned red and he stomped out of the garage.

When he had calmed down, I offered a further thought. "It doesn't really matter whether you are able to ride by the time we go camping," I proposed, "though it might be nice to set a goal. Then we could practice each day until we leave on our trip."

Still no go, though this time minus the drama at least.

Bribery Backfires—Celebrate Instead

I need to tell you that I don't like to bribe my kids, especially with food. When children are bribed to do things, they learn to perform only for the reward, not for the intrinsic enjoyment of doing something. It sets a bad precedent for how they will function in adult life. So when I share with you what I did, I don't want you to think of it as bribery.

In our house, candy is an extremely rare treat. If there

was something that would help my son brave his fear—
something that would excite him sufficiently to at least give
it a go—I sensed that the promise of a candy bar was the
most likely thing to do the trick. With this in mind, I
suggested that, once he could ride on his own, it might be
fun for us to celebrate. "We'll get you a full-sized candy
bar all for yourself," I promised.

Bingo—we had an agreement.

The deal was that Brady would practice riding for just
five minutes each day. This was a gentle challenge,
nothing too ambitious, designed not to scare him. I made
sure to tell myself to stop the practice before he tired,
which might lead to him falling down. A fall would have
ended his willingness to work toward our goal. Whereas
parents often want to push their children just that bit
further, egging them on, I've learned the value of a more
conservative approach. This allows children to set their
own limits should they choose to do more.

Notice that I couched the candy bar in terms of a
"celebration." There's a huge qualitative difference
between manipulating a child, such as by bribing them to
do something we want them to do but that they really
don't want to do, and celebrating an achievement they
themselves are trying to bring about. The feel is quite
dissimilar, and it's important to make this abundantly clear
should you at any time choose to use this technique.

The first day we went out, Brady rode quite well,
though still insisting he didn't want me to let go of the
back of his bike. We stuck to our timeline, and that night I
told him how proud I was of him for working at the goal
we had set for ourselves.

Children are all very, very different, so that parenting can never be based on a one-size-fits-all template. Brady is the kind of kid who needs time to think about things, processing them in his own manner. That night, as he was falling asleep—which is a time when he tends to mull things over—he clearly allowed himself to "feel into" this experience.

The second day, my brave little fellow announced, "I want you to hold my bike, Mom. But let go when I say so." I agreed. He took a deep breath, then began to pedal. As he did so, I experienced an overwhelming sense of just how hard he was working to overcome his fear.

After a little while he shouted, "Okay, let go!" When I did so, he managed to peddle a few feet further before beginning to wobble, whereupon I grabbed the back of his bike seat to steady him. Wow, was that ever a mistake! When he realized I was assisting him with his balance, he got mad, letting me know in no uncertain terms he didn't want me holding onto the bike after he had said to let go.

Why did I jump in to rescue him? Simply because I allowed my own fear to intrude. I was afraid that if he fell off, especially if he hurt himself, the bike riding would have been nixed. With such a setback, who knows when he would ever learn to ride on his own?

If we want to help our children overcome their fear, we have to model living free of fear. We can't allow our overprotectiveness as parents to get the better of us, as I did that day. It's very much a dance, whereby we encourage our children to step out on their own, and in a sense even gently push them, while being there for them to return to us for reassurance when *they* seek it.

On the next attempt, I did exactly what Brady asked of me, letting go and simply following behind. Again beginning to wobble, it looked as though he was about to topple off; however, thankfully he had the presence of mind to put his foot down and save himself. I could feel waves of fear emanating from him, and yet I also saw how, despite how scared he was, he was determined to once and for all learn to ride his bike. This was the first time I had ever seen such resolve in him.

After three more attempts, when I let go once more, suddenly he was off and riding. I felt a thrill, a feeling of elation I can scarcely describe. It was exhilarating to see my child finally claim this rite of passage.

The Illusion of Fear

At bedtime that evening, Brady confessed he had had to work hard to overcome his fear of riding his bike. We talked about how he had found his courage that day, extrapolating this to how, whenever he felt scared from now on, he could always remember back to this moment and draw encouragement from it.

Fear is like the boogie man, holding us in its spell. It's a mirage that totally fools us. However, once we actually confront it, it simply evaporates as I saw so clearly now from the way, as soon as Brady knew he could do it, he in no time looked so comfortable on that bicycle saddle, as if he had been riding for years.

During the following week, Brady was on his bike every day. Of course, the bike came to camp with us, and since that time we have taken family bike rides and traveled for miles. I had so looked forward to all of us taking bike rides together. Having waited so many years for all three of my kids to become independent bike riders, the realization of this dream felt like Christmas to me.

I had initially wanted Brady to ride his bike when he was four, like his brother Noah. Of course, as so many parents do, I could have forced him to practice every day until he got it. But we would both have been miserable. This was neither the approach I wanted to take, nor the way I wanted our relationship to be.

To parent effectively is to go at a child's own pace. So even though it took Brady longer than it takes other kids, in his own time he officially became a bicyclist. But far more important was what, in the process of mastering his pedals, he learned about his capacity for courage.

Parents so often want to rush their kids from one challenge to the next, as if they had to collect badges of honor on a societally defined schedule. Not only do the children not get to bask in their achievements, exploring the feelings they had to surmount to achieve their accomplishment, but neither do the rest of the family get to luxuriate in the fact a child has reached a milestone.

The couple of weeks that followed this triumph happened to be somewhat laid back and slower for our family, which afforded me an opportunity to savor this benchmark in Brady's little life and mine. I was mindful to bask in and absorb the joy I found in my son's victory.

This was one of those parenting moments that are so rich, so fulfilling, I sensed it held within it the power to support me through the more difficult challenges that inevitably occur in the course of a child's development. If we allow such moments the space to do so, they nourish our soul, equipping us to cope with the tougher times. How sad it is that so many of us rush through our days and don't take the opportunity to relish these moments for the gift they are.

Give Your Children Space to Do It Themselves

Because of his different temperament, Brady has taught me much about parenting. For instance, when he was seven, he went to his first cub scout camp. For the most part he was excited to spend the week with his friends. I say "for the most part" because, as I mentioned earlier, he's usually wary of unfamiliar experiences.

Talk about how fun the camp activities would be triggered from Brady a decisive declaration that one activity he *wasn't* going to be participating in was swimming. Not because he didn't know how to swim—quite the opposite. He's been on a competitive swim team since he was four, which likely qualified him as the strongest and most capable swimmer in his group.

In the days leading up to the start of camp, he announced several times that he wouldn't be swimming in the lake. Knowing him as well as I do, I let the comments pass instead of getting into a protracted discussion.

When the day arrived that our group walked to the lake for the swim session, Brady refused to change into his bathing suit. He just sat there on the bench, declining to swim. His good friend came over and suggested he take the harder swim test, since he's such a good swimmer—a proposal Brady didn't so much as dignify with an answer. The entire time the other boys swam and enjoyed themselves, he simply sat watching them.

We talked in an earlier chapter about moms wanting to be perfect, or at least to be seen as such. So you'll understand when I tell you that not only was my blood boiling, but my heart was also breaking for Brady as I observed him sitting all alone. The thoughts that raced through my head ran something like, "I know he's the strongest swimmer in the group. For the life of me, I can't begin to fathom why he wouldn't want to swim with all his friends. Look at what he's missing out on. This is terrible!" As moms, do we ever get beyond having such feelings well up inside us at times like this?

It so happened that I had been making a study of how to parent consciously, which allowed me to acknowledge the emotions that were exploding in me but not act them out. I allowed myself to feel how annoying it was, not to mention wildly uncomfortable for me as a go-getter myself, to watch my son refuse to dive into a new experience. At the same time, I was careful to keep my focus on merely observing what I was feeling in a detached and nonreactive manner, instead of spewing it out onto Brady.

Understanding Brady the way I do, I realized he needs time to warm up to new experiences, which can mean he eventually may or may not end up participating. One thing was for certain: if I pushed him, there was no way he would participate. On top of this, we would end up disconnected because I would be angry and he would feel neither supported, heard, nor understood.

I'll come back to this incident with my son in a moment, but at this point I want to share that I'm currently working with a foster mom who has a menagerie of children in her care, consisting of a biological daughter, an adopted daughter and son, three foster daughters, and one foster son. This loving mom works extremely hard to help all these kids from different families to blend into a single family under her roof. Her efforts are always well intended; however, they don't always have a good outcome, and the issue I was dealing with in the case of my own son and swimming at the lake touches on the reason for this.

This mother decided to surprise the children by telling them they would all be going to a light show together the coming weekend. The fifteen year old foster son was extremely annoyed by this news and declared that he just wanted to be left alone, free to hang out with his friends. The mother insisted he participated in this outing in order to develop family cohesiveness. Instead of cohesiveness, what forcing the boy to go to the light show accomplished was to build resentment and further his desire to break away.

I could completely sympathize with this mom's intentions, but her plan failed to honor what was very important to her foster son. Peers are extremely important to a fifteen year old, and trying to force him to do something he didn't want to do away from his peers could only result in further disconnection.

In order to develop a deeper connection in the long run, sometimes we have to choose the option we might not prefer at the time. If this mother had allowed her foster son to stay at his friend's house while the rest of the group went to the light show—and enjoyed themselves—imagine how their relationship might have looked the next day.

In my own son's case, I did make a few missteps, and I'm thankful it's acceptable for us parents to make mistakes without feeling we have blown our children's upbringing. My missteps? Twice during the swim session, I went over to my son and calmly asked him if he was going to end up swimming that day. The first time, he simply said "no." The second time, he became so angry that he gritted his teeth and seethed, "If you don't stop asking me, I am not going to want to live with you anymore."

That's when I knew to back off. So I let him sit there by himself, taking the opportunity to walk to a bench where I too could sit by myself.

A few minutes later, when he had calmed himself down, he came over and put his arms around my waist. Hugging him, I told him I was feeling sad because something was preventing him from swimming with his friends, and I wished we could figure out what it was.

Timing is everything, as they say. Since he seemed receptive at this moment, I asked him a series of questions: "Are you scared you won't pass the swim test? Are you afraid everyone will look at you? Are you fearful your friends will expect you to be the best swimmer? Do you not like that it's a lake and not a pool? Do you not like the sand on the bottom of the lake?"

When his response to each of my questions was that this wasn't the problem, I confided that I had run out of ideas. "We can keep talking about it if you want to try to figure this out," I offered. But he declined and walked back to his bench to sit alone once more. Using my smarts this time, I didn't follow him

When the swim session ended, two of his friends came over and asked him why he didn't swim. No response.

When the lifeguard lined all the boys up and passed out beads to those who participated, he mistakenly handed one to Brady. Jumping in, I interjected, "He needs to give the bead back, since he didn't participate." Then, realizing I had made yet another misstep, I qualified what I said in an attempt to ameliorate the situation. "Maybe Brady will swim tomorrow," I proposed, trying to sound hopeful. The lifeguard took the bead back and continued down the line.

Brady was crushed. All he could do was stand in line with his friends, holding his head in his hands so they wouldn't see him crying. I felt so bad. I wanted to run over and "make it all better" for him, but I knew he needed to work through this experience, and so I hung back and allowed it to unfold. Finally pulling himself together, he walked to the next activity.

At bedtime that night, Brady asked, "Would I have to take the swim test just to go ankle deep in the first part of the lake?"

"I'm not sure," I replied, "but we could ask the lifeguard." As usual at bedtime, he was processing his problem. Shortly thereafter he fell asleep.

When morning came, he decided to dress in his swimsuit rather than shorts "just in case." I smiled but was careful not to say anything. When we arrived at the lake, he pulled off his shirt and ran to jump in the lake with the rest of his friends. Whatever had been holding my little guy back had been overcome.

As it was, I made enough mistakes dealing with this

situation. Had such a scenario arisen prior to my PCI parent coach training, or before reading *The Child Whisperer*, *The Conscious Parent* and *Out of Control*, I would have forced the issue, cajoling and manipulating Brady into swimming that first day. The motivation for this? Purely my own anxiety about him not participating and missing out. The day would have ended with both of us upset with each other and a major disconnect.

Maya Angelou said she had learned that people will forget what you said, and forget what you did, but never forget how you made them feel. In years to come, my son likely won't remember whether he swam four days or five at cub scout camp, but he will always remember feeling loved, supported, and connected to me. He'll also remember having a lake-full of fun with his friends.

CHAPTER 16

Parenting Is a Learning Process

"IT'S OKAY, MOMMY, I forgive you," said my daughter Faith. "I still love you, even when you are angry. You have to always remember that." As she spoke, she looked deep into my eyes. Then, when she followed up her reassuring words by giving me a big hug, it melted all the tension that had accumulated during the past two days, and I felt a wave of gratitude for my precious little girl.

Next I went to Noah's room to talk with him. Since he's older and in the throes of puberty, when I apologized to him for my crabbiness the last few days, I explained what hormonal imbalance can do to females from the onset of puberty and well up into their adult years. I shared with him how it can result in sadness, impatience, anger, and other unhelpful emotions.

"I understand," he responded in his usual wise way. "I kind of knew this was what was going on anyway, because" at this point, a sly half-grin creased his face "there's no way you could have been that mad at me for a legitimate reason."

It felt good to have things back to normal around the house. I also perceived that I was even more connected to each of my children than I usually was because of the mature way in which they had consciously navigated my difficult behavior.

My apology had come on the heels of a couple of bad days that had caused me to reflect. Leading up to this apology, I had dropped my kids off at swim practice and found myself wanting to take a few quiet minutes alone in my car to ponder what had transpired. I also wanted to write about my experience, which always helps to bring clarity to whatever may be going on inside of me. After this brief interval of reflection, I could feel my hormones returning to their more usual balance. It was like waking up and observing the early morning fog lift from my brain.

Following swim practice, as Faith and Brady were getting their things together to leave the pool, I sat back and quietly listened to how kind and helpful they were being to each other. A wave of gratitude passed through me. Despite the fact I hadn't modeled kindness the last couple of days, their sweet energy toward each other filled me with joy, and I knew that what we had been through had been nothing but an aberration. It wasn't the way we live in our family from day to day.

Reflection Brings Reassurance

We were in the dog days of summer. Since the kids were out of school, this was my busiest time of year. However, as the days roll into one another and there was no letup in the demands on me, one afternoon a pocket of time magically opened up for me.

148

Instead of spending this serendipitous afternoon cleaning, paying bills, and preparing dinner, I took a few minutes to sit down and reflect on just how challenging it can be to try to work from home during the summer. As already mentioned, I find that reflection is a powerful tool for evaluating and redirecting my expenditure of energy toward those aspects of life where it can best be utilized.

The week had seen a dramatic decrease in the craziness of my family's schedule. My daughter had finished up three weeks of daylong theater camp, culminating in six performances over three days the previous week. My younger son had spent full days at cub scout camp that same previous week. Now, the only one in camp was my older child, for whom band camp took up a portion of each day.

Camp days had proved to be a trying time, making it difficult to get my own work done in my job as a counselor, let alone finding time to attend to my business, It Takes A Village Parent Coaching. During the time the kids were all in camp, I had spent my days driving them to and fro instead of working. However, if I imagined having them mostly home now that camp was mostly over would make things easier, I was mistaken. The issues were different, but equally challenging. I might be doing less driving, but I had three kids wandering around trying to find something, or someone, to occupy them.

When my children are in school, my days are tightly organized, which enables me to work not only in counseling and in my business, but also to keep our home running. As summer arrives, I'm still required to do all these things, except with little time during which my children are all occupied and not in need of my attention.

Of course, as so many parents do, I could take the easy road and allow unlimited access to screens in the form of video games, phones, computers, and television. However, that's not my way, since I don't believe it's for my children's good which, as a mom of three children growing up in a very tech-driven society, creates an even bigger challenge.

Principles for Busy Parents

No two working parents face quite the same challenges, but there are some principles that are valid across the board. In addition to being aware of these, it comes down to the choices we are willing to make so that we honor our own working life while also respecting the needs of our family. If we ignore these principles and continually make choices that generate additional stress, we do so not only at our own peril but also that of our children.

My situation is a little different from that of many working mothers in that I'm not required to work full-time. When I say "required," I need to share that this is the result of a choice my husband and I made together. Whereas I see other working parents opting for the large house in a prestigious neighborhood, a flashy car, and a membership at the country club, we prepared for these years when our children were going to need me by working hard to adopt a more minimalist, less consumer-driven lifestyle. Still, even without working full-time, there are things that need to be attended to, especially with respect to my parent coaching.

I think, too, one never completely escapes the kind of conflict over wanting to work if one loves one's work, while also desiring to spend time with the children. I find that part of me yearns to dive headlong into my work. On the other hand, as a mindful and conscious parent, I also like to spend quality time with my offspring while they are young, for I know that years later I would regret not doing so. I'm acutely cognizant of the fact that this particular phase of their lives happens but once; it's not like we can revisit it whenever we at last have the time. Since I value, and indeed relish, all the aspects of my life as a working mother, I sometimes can't help but wish there were more hours in each day, especially when school is out for the summer.

I mentioned principles that can help. Whether we work full-time or part-time, it's important to monitor and adjust for the craziness that can so easily rule our lives as working parents. This involves making the tough decision not to stretch ourselves too thin.

If we love each aspect of our life, it's inevitable we're going to want to take on too much. But this is where an awareness of our finitude needs to be brought to bear on our choices. Pacing ourselves, it's vital to balance our activity instead of saying "yes" to every request. Thus an essential aspect of parenting is the ability to utter a definitive "no" to some things, tears and wailing notwithstanding, and simply ride out the storm in a state of equanimity. Equally, we need to judiciously elect to involve ourselves in those activities that best serve the interest of everyone, saying a decisive "yes" to those we opt for, then giving them our all.

In this equation, it's essential to carve out time for our own self-care. If we wish to give of ourselves to others, both at work and with our children, not to mention a significant other, we need to ensure our own bucket stays full. For me this is a priority, and you've been seeing all along how I value time alone, time to write, and time to reflect.

Another principle is the importance of being flexible, including where possible seeking assistance rather than trying to do it all ourselves. Humans are creatures of habit, which means it's easy for us to lapse into a fixed way of doing things and not even give thought to whether there might be a need for a change.

To illustrate, in the evenings my husband and I customarily catch up on the day's events, then enjoy relaxing for a while with a movie or perhaps an episode of Oprah's Super Soul Sunday, depending on our mood. However, with the added challenge of the kids needing my attention in the summer, this past summer I found it necessary to devote one evening a week, after the children were in bed, to working on my business. To be able to focus for several uninterrupted hours is immensely helpful. Along with this, I schedule one or two calls a week with my colleague to do business planning. These calls are usually scheduled early in the morning, just after I've fed my kids breakfast and before we dive into our activities for the day. Additionally, one day a week my mother-in-law comes to spend the day with the children, which enables me to attend my counseling job.

Children, too, need principles to guide them through the summers. My children understand that, for the most part, the mornings are to be spent free from friends, engaging in what I refer to as mind-expanding activities, which basically means screen-free imaginative play, math worksheets, reading, building with Legos, constructing forts, and so on. If we are home, afternoons are free for some screen-time, swimming, and playing with friends.

Life Is a Trade-off

So that I'm not interrupted, my kids are learning to be quiet when I'm on a work call. In return for their respect for my needs, when I'm free later, I devote my time to being with them in whatever activity they are engaged in.

For example, earlier one afternoon, after I finished up some work for the day, my twelve-year-old wanted to play chess, so we got the chessboard out for an hour. Although my phone was beeping with messages, I intentionally kept it away from me so I could give him my undivided attention. It was important that nothing get in the way of our interaction. While we challenged each other with knights, bishops, and queens, my two younger kids were playing at their friends' house down the street. After chess, I agreed that Noah could engage in some video game time, sticking to Madden football and not the more violent video games, none of which we own. While he was playing this game, I had a chance to sit down and write.

Whereas during the school year I aim to go to the gym four times a week, I only managed to get to the gym once during the first week school was out. I was okay with this, since I realize I have to be more flexible in the summer.

However, I'm careful to compensate for the times I miss, since I deem a moderate amount of exercise a vital aspect of a healthy life. For one thing, it helps balance those hormones I talked about earlier.

To illustrate how I compensate, one particular day, knowing I wouldn't make it to the gym, while my older son was in band camp I took my two younger kids and our dog on a long walk despite the heat. This gave us all some much-needed exercise, and as a result we each felt better. A good walk has so many benefits, not only for our health but for lifting our spirits, fostering camaraderie, and helping us feel a part of the natural world that's our own mother.

My mantra is to fit life in, where I can, how I can. This requires mindfulness. I find that if we are aware, we find ways to adjust so that our children receive the time and attention they deserve, while we also identify small windows in which to complete our grownup tasks. Again, it's a matter of flexibility. Yes, I love to have a number of uninterrupted hours to write, for example; but I've also learned I can begin a piece while sitting in my car for several minutes.

It comes back to the matter of balance, which I mentioned a little while ago. Whenever I feel stressed, I realize something is off kilter. Rather than giving into the stress and becoming upset, then starting to complain and growing increasingly critical, I find a few precious moments to reflect. This allows me to figure out where the lack of balance is occurring.

I would be remiss if I didn't make it clear that there's always pressure on parents to do more, which automatically feeds our tendency to feel inadequate as a person, let alone as a parent. The sense of inadequacy that accompanies parenting is par for the course. For this reason, it's quite foolish to scold or punish ourselves at the behest of our inner critic. It's far preferable to simply embrace the fact we will always tend to feel that we "aren't doing enough."

No Perfect Parent

Lots of us would like to be the perfect parent, I think especially mothers. Perhaps we fancy ourselves as the mom all the kids in the neighborhood gravitate to—the cookie baker, the lemonade maker, the girl scout leader, the girls' soccer coach, the one who hosts sleepovers, the perfect party thrower—you list the endless "perfect mom" attributes.

Of course, our nails are all the while immaculate, our hair in place, our makeup done to perfection, as we entertain a gaggle of youngsters.

On the one hand we hear the aphorism, "Nobody's perfect." Yet on the other hand, the ideal of perfection runs deep in our culture, perhaps because for so long we've heard in the Sermon on the Mount how Jesus said, "Be ye therefore perfect, even as your heavenly father is perfect."

Except that this isn't what Jesus said. The Greek word means "complete," or "mature," which is a fundamentally different concept from what we think of as "perfection." Think of a mature plant. It's a plant that's grown into the lettuce, the rose, the cabbage, the oak tree it was intended to be. When this statement by Jesus entered the English language more than four centuries ago, even the English word "perfect" didn't mean what it does today, but had this sense of being "mature."

So what is a mature person? Maturity is the art of being able to hold life's many facets in balance, maintaining a state of inner harmony when situations pull us first one way, then another. There will always be a host of forces tugging on us as working parents—it's unavoidable. The mature person accepts this, while simultaneously embracing the ambivalence they feel at times.

Especially when the kids are out of school for the summer, I confess that sometimes it feels a lot like being a juggler, as I attempt to keep many balls in the air. The question is, can I be okay with this? If I give myself permission to mess up, and keep consciously adjusting where an adjustment can help smooth things along the way, I find life as a working mother is a lot less difficult.

Trying to be perfect is a tense state. Instead of being perfectly okay with being an imperfect person, you are constantly trying to earn Brownie points. With that frame of mind, you never really relax and just "be." Even when you finally get to park your carcass in front of the television with pretzels and a glass of wine, a soda, or a cup of tea or mug of coffee, you're still not relaxed. Immobile, but not relaxed not on inside. Tensed shoulders, taut vocal chords, a tight chest, and a knotted stomach all tell the truth. As does how very little it takes to irritate many of us.

When we feel we ought to be perfect, we go through life expecting things to be perfect. When they aren't, we're miserable. Expecting perfection of situations, and of ourselves is a recipe for misery. It causes us to block all enjoyment of the moment because we have a concept of how things ought to be and when they aren't that way, we're fit to be tied.

You've been into those buildings in which security cameras are always moving, blinking, picking up any kind of motion, registering any potential threat. Because we have this ingrained belief that we ought to be doing better, this is what it's like for many of us all the time. Our security system is never down. We're always monitoring to see whether things are perfect enough, whether we're measuring up, whether others are pulling their weight.

I submit that what we really want isn't perfection, which is a silly and quite boring notion. What we want is to be fully engaged, whereby we feel each experience with our whole being.

When you enter into the pure feeling of any situation, you feel "okayed." Yes, I coined this word, because what I'm trying to express isn't simply that we are okay. To be "okayed" is to feel in your chest, your neck, your back, your stomach that you are lovable. And to be lovable is to be love-*able*. Finding yourself okayed, you find others okay too. Now you can handle life's ambiguities, its ups and downs, it sheer rapture and it's at times horrific disappointments. You can embrace your ambivalence toward certain aspects of life. But most of all, you can simply enjoy.

I can't tell you the world of difference between struggling all the time to feel perfect, and simply enjoying the feeling of just *being*, with all of its dichotomies and complexities, its enigmas and paradoxes. Really, when you think about trying to be perfect, it's comic. No one, absolutely no one, can pull it off. So why do we try?

A felt sense of ourselves as "okayed" by life is the strong lens we all really long to peer through, not the weak lens of imagining we can somehow be perfect. It's about seeing our life through softer eyes. With this new set of lenses, each moment is felt strongly and embraced fully. Free of all attempts to make it perfect, life becomes pregnant with possibility.

CHAPTER 17

Parenting from the Bright Side:
We CAN End School Shootings

I ADMIT IT. I am a self-proclaimed optimist—in fact, a die-hard optimist to be precise. Most people who know me would describe me this way as well, so it's not just an image I hold of myself.

In this light, I've been thinking and thinking about the escalating number of school shootings and what can be done to stop them. The problem is so complex. Quite apart from the actual shootings, we are facing a veritable tidal wave of bullying that we seem powerless to restrain.

If we are ever to stop violence on our campuses, serious change needs to occur at the federal level, in the states, and in municipalities across the nation—change so sweeping that it's almost too overwhelming to contemplate it. For instance, change needs to occur in the mental health arena, as well as in education. It needs to occur in the judicial division, which affects so many parents and children. The changes that are needed are all huge in scope, requiring not only time but a willingness of people to come together to generate ideas and inspiration, all of which must be followed up with concrete action.

Technology isn't going to be the answer, no matter how much schools invest in wonderful inventions that can help keep kids safe in their classrooms. Where lasting change needs to take place, technology can only ever treat the symptom, not the root cause.

How to Take Effective Action

Because the problem of school violence is overwhelming, let's try thinking smaller. Since most of us can't directly impact society's structures, what can each of us do—starting right this minute—to take some small step in the right direction, a step that hopefully will generate a ripple effect that grows bigger and bigger?

In my own life, the place I've made a start is to be more conscious of the way I treat others. Whether we are aware of it or not, I believe we respond to each other on an energetic level. How often are we rushed, stressed, and harried as we race from one activity, one task, to another? The problem is that when we rush like this, the emotional backlash it awakens in us tends to get taken out on our loved ones. They feel the brunt of our frustration. Or maybe we are curt with the gas station attendant because we had to wait in line, or with the waitress who forgot we didn't want tomatoes on our sandwich.

How many times have you responded to someone in a less than kind way, or witnessed someone responding to someone in an unkind manner? Think about it for a moment. It's a pretty frequent occurrence in many of our lives, don't you think?

Now, imagine if each of us, starting this minute, became aware of the way we treat people, then set an intention to actively increase the kindness we show others. What would the world look like if we each made this small change?

Why does this matter? How can it really change things? Well, let me ask you, how often have we learned that the shooter in one of our school's tragedies was shunned by his classmates, didn't have friends, and was essentially a loner? You can bet that not too many people showed kindness to any of the individuals who have committed these atrocities.

If a person who feels isolated is treated with decency and respect as a regular occurrence, how many lives might be saved? I believe that for people to be kind to one another, especially in our schools, would be a huge step forward. It's not so easy to shoot people if you are close to them and feel as though you are one of them.

We may not be able to change the essential structures of society, such as the educational system and the courts, overnight, but the way we treat people, especially those teetering on the edge, is something we have the power to change today.

A Practical Suggestion to Increase the Kindness in Society

One of the steps we could take toward a kinder society is to slow down. We have to relieve the stress we all place on ourselves, in addition to the stress the system places on us. I come in contact with so many whose schedules are far too hectic and who, because they are overcommitted, feel drained of energy. When this is your basic state, you have little left for kindness.

Life doesn't have to be lived this way. *You* don't have to live this way. Many of us would find our days so much more enjoyable, as well as rewarding, if we simplified our lifestyle with less "stuff" in our closets and fewer events on our calendars, allowing us the mental space to begin to spread a little kindness.

Do I need to say that it begins with being kind to ourselves? It can be difficult to be kind to others if we are beating ourselves up for our own shortcomings, our presumed inefficiency, our failure to meet our targets. If your inner critic is having a heyday, give yourself a break from all that self-criticism. Missing a goal or even messing up, needs to be seen not as a failure of who we are but as a learning experience to call forth more of the intrinsically wonderful individual each of us is.

Have you ever noticed how much people complain about the state of things when they get together with others? The government, the economy, immigration issues, crime—we can all find things to criticize. But unless we are actually going to do something about these issues, and our discussion revolves around the action we are proposing, what good is achieved by all our complaining?

This may sound corny, but when we count our blessings when we take the time to look around and feel grateful for a sunrise, a hug, a smile, or the rainfall that waters our gardens we spread the kind of vibes, the kind of energy, that can lift everyone.

A thankful person, radiating gratitude everywhere they

go, is a powerful antidote to the fear, gloom, isolation, and negativity that hold so many of us captive. Of course, if only a handful of us radiate such thankfulness, we may not see big results. But if there's a sufficient ripple effect, the world will become a significantly happier place to live. We aren't powerless to change things, and I for one am optimistic it can happen.

The Downsides of an Overemphasis on Sports

Were I to pick one single facet of life in which a positive, rather than a negative, approach would make a world of difference in terms of how our children treat one another—whether they show kindness to one another, cheering each other on, including one another in activities––it would be sports. Despite its many benefits, this aspect of our educational and social systems, at least as we know it now, constitutes one of the most negative influences our culture has on our children when it comes to promoting hostility.

As a school year ends, one generally expects it to be the end of another season of sport. But with today's hard-driving emphasis on youth sports, seasons don't seem to draw to a close like they once did. Official swimming classes may be over, and there may be no more dance performances. Despite this, for many sports such as soccer, basketball, baseball, swimming, and football, seasons go almost year-round, overlapping one other to the point that our young people are in many cases either playing or practicing for multiple sports at a time. And I'm not just talking about at the high school level, but about kids as young as seven.

In terms of fostering a spirit of kindness in young people, I have some issues with the overemphasis on sport, even from a purely practical point of view. Not least of my concerns is the increased risk of repetitive motion injuries. Young children's bones and ligaments are still growing, which makes performing the same range of motions over and over without respite nothing less than dangerous. Even the American Academy of Pediatrics says that up to 50% of all injuries seen in pediatric sports medicine are due to overuse injuries, although the reality is that overuse injuries are just the tip of the iceberg.

The American Academy of Pediatrics also describes something called "overtraining syndrome," which it categories as a "series of psychological, physiologic, and hormonal changes that result in decreased sports performance." Common manifestations of this syndrome may include chronic muscle or joint pain, personality changes, an elevated resting heart rate, and decreased sports performance. The pediatric athlete may also experience fatigue, lack of enthusiasm with respect to practice or competition, and difficulty with successfully completing common routines.

Burnout should also be recognized as a serious consequence of overtraining syndrome. However, this is a simple problem to fix. Prevention of burnout can be accomplished by encouraging athletes to become well rounded. Not only does being versed in a variety of activities, rather than being focused on one particular sport, help protect from injury, but it has a significant effect on an individual's spirit.

Can you believe that burnout is a real issue for our kids? A phenomenon we usually associate with syndromes such as midlife crisis, it's hard to believe that it occurs with increasing frequency among our youngsters. However, I personally have seen many extremely talented athletes walk away from a sport they previously loved because they pushed themselves too hard, or were pushed by their parents or a coach, to the point they no longer enjoy their chosen sport.

What Are We Teaching Our Kids?

Injury and burnout are only two of the negative results of an overemphasis on sports, and both of them result primarily from the aggressive attitude we promote. It's this attitude that spills over into the playground, the classroom, and just about every aspect of how kids relate to one another. They learn to be hostile to one another instead of kind.

Former NFL player Damian Vaughn, whose overexertion led to an injury that put him out of the game, highlights the deleterious effect of what he calls a "Darwinian" approach to sport, contrasted with what he refers to as "playing from the soul." He cites a statement crayoned on a blackboard mounted on the wall of a bedroom he was sleeping in while visiting a buddy who had three young boys, two of whom were in college and the other still in high school. In answer to the question of why he loved football, the boy had written on the blackboard,

"So I can be popular, get girls and hitting people *feels* good."

What intrigued Vaughn was the fact that the boy's rationale for playing football had nothing to do with actually loving the sport in and of itself. What happened to playing for the sheer love of a sport, the exhilaration, the enjoyment?

Vaughn explains that approaching life in this Darwinian "beat others down" mentality generates an unbalanced internal state. The athlete's body then experiences a correlated neurological response of nervousness and anxiety. As this dysfunctional internal state ripples into the outside world, it manifests as hostility during play and drama in everyday life, particularly in relationships. It's the reason so many sports figures, despite the fact they are regarded as champions and heroes in the arena, have disastrous personal lives.

So how can we, as a culture, inspire greatness in our young athletes?

If we want to inspire greatness, kindness rules. And the first feature of its reign needs to be that as adults guiding our young people, we *compliment* them rather than *criticize*. On far too many occasions, I have observed coaches and even more often, parents berate a young person the moment they can get to them after the child has messed up in a game or competition.

I've also seen solid, star athletes of all ages crack under the pressure of a highly competitive game. But what's really concerning is that on every single occasion when this has happened, there was a parent on the sidelines waiting to rip into their child as they came off the field. One misplay is all it takes to bring down many a parent's ire.

Am I talking about a particular sport? Far from it. This happens over and over in every kind of sport. It's also principally parents who have turned games like soccer into a sport with a lot of pushing and shoving, something that simply didn't happen in the more wholesome days of soccer. Many adults actually *advocate* trying to injure a player on the opposite team in a sport so they can take them out of the game. What happened to playing for the fun of it, as well as to develop one's skills to a superior level? Knocking others out of the game just to win militates against developing superlative skills, since all you are doing is eliminating the challenge.

A Good Coach Makes All the Difference

Coaches are in the most advantageous position to be able to change the spirit of the game, whereby a sport becomes a means of excelling rather than a form of warfare in which opponents try to destroy each other.

That said, it's important to recognize that, even where a coach is concerned, the ultimate power lies with parents, who are also uniquely positioned in that they can directly influence not only their offspring but also the hiring and firing of coaches. If there's anywhere kindness needs to prevail, it's on the court, in the arena, and on the playing field. Playing to enjoy and excel is the name of the game. Including those who tend to stay on the sidelines, so that they feel part of a team, is vital. Coaches, backed by caring parents, are the key to this becoming a reality.

Long ago, an excellent coach encouraged me to ask my children following a game, race, or competition, whether they had fun. Did they enjoy themselves? Our youngsters are much more likely to want to continue participating in activities they enjoy. They are also less likely to overstress themselves as they approach the next competition.

I have to thank Rachel Macy Stafford for the pearl of wisdom she handed me when she suggested I tell my kids, "I love to watch you play." When was the last time you said nothing about *how* your daughter or son played, but instead told them how much you loved to watch them play?

A statement of this nature goes a long way to shaping the perspective of our kids. My children's eyes light up each and every time I tell them how much I enjoy watching them play. However, what if we were also to tell even fringe players, or those on the opposing team, that we enjoy watching them? What might this do for building the kind of camaraderie that inoculates against campus violence?

I want you to know that when I say this, I mean it. I want to support all children in a game, and I truly don't care whether my kids win or lose. My greatest thrill comes from watching them participate in the activities they love, while bonding with their peers as they do so. I also recognize that if they are enjoying what they are doing, as well as feeling good about themselves while they do it, they will be more relaxed, which is the optimum way for their skills to improve. Kindness is great fertilizer for the honing of skills.

If the Shoe Fits

It's important to recognize when a sport isn't right for a particular child. This is poignantly brought out in the 2000 movie Billy Elliot, which is about a young boy growing up in northern England whose father wanted him to be a boxer. Billy desired something entirely different for himself. To his father's shock and horror, he wanted to be a ballet dancer. The film is well worth watching as an aid to understanding the importance of allowing our children each to blossom according to their own bent. The story has also become one of the most celebrated award-winning musicals on the stage, selling out in London on a nightly basis and from there spreading to theaters around the world, including Broadway.

The lesson of Billy Elliot, which while fictional mirrors the lives of many who have climbed to the top against all odds, is that our role is merely to expose our children to sports. Beyond this, they need to be allowed to exercise their preferences. It's not our job as parents to push them into a particular sport, to pressure them to excel, or even to urge them to take up a sport at all. It's far kinder to follow *their* lead, supporting them to go as far as they wish to. If a child's life is going to involve a particular sport, sooner or later the child will figure this out.

That being said, when my youngest was seven, his team won their baseball championship game. Though he wasn't the star player on the team by a long shot, and perhaps closer to the weakest player than the strongest, it was of little account. What mattered was that every practice and every game, my little guy went out there and worked hard.

He focused well and did everything his coaches asked him to do. So even though he didn't hit a home run, I was proud of him. To work hard and exercise determination are important life skills, and all that matters to me is that, deep inside himself, he knows this.

It so happened that the same weekend my first grader's team won the baseball championship, he also successfully read his first *Magic Tree House* book by himself, and he did it in two days. Now that's something to celebrate, as well as something that will take him far in life.

This being the case, the greatest kindness I can show my son is to allow him to play his chosen sports for the fun of it, while restraining myself from all temptation to rate sports as more important than they really are. When a love of the game, coupled with an inclusive and benevolent attitude toward other students, predominates, the incidence of hostility on campuses can't help but diminish. There will be less and less fringe individuals who feel a need to strike out against their fellow pupils, whether from feeling alienated or in order to make their distorted mark on the world.

Where Sportsmanship Begins

From my experience, if anyone needs to learn sportsmanship, it's parents. Boy, did I see a lot of poor sportsmanship from my age group this season. I witnessed it from parents whose children's teams were winning, as well as from parents whose children's teams were losing.

To be on the losing team is difficult enough for our

kids, without parents from the opposite side gloating about their victory as if *they* had been the ones on the field. Something far more important than winning is at stake, involving our children's self-understanding both individually and collectively.

At the same time as parents need to refrain from gloating, they also need to steer away from finding excuses for why their child's team lost. If there are two players in a sport, or two teams, one of them *has* to lose. Our role as parents is to encourage our kids to win graciously as well as lose graciously, for they will "win" and "lose" at many things beyond sports over the course of their lives. Learning how to come through situations with grace and dignity is an important aspect of growing up, and it all begins with how children see us conducting ourselves. In other words, the way to teach good sportsmanship is by modeling it.

As with ancient Rome's gladiators at the Coliseum, it's all too easy in our modern world, with our mass electronic spectatorship, to relate greatness to the field, the arena, or the court. Yet it's not in sports but in the ordinary activities of life that the rubber meets the road. Sports need to impart lessons and principles that carry over into daily activities and thereby prove valuable for decades to come.

This became particularly clear to me one winter when my oldest son had a basketball coach who my husband and I agreed was the best volunteer parent coach we had ever seen across all ages and sports. Coach Ricky was fantastic. My son had returned to basketball that winter after deciding of his own accord to take a year off. Quite randomly, he ended up on a team that had only a few good players, with the majority average or below average. Some were even first-time players. So how did this team, playing in a fairly competitive bracket, win the championship?

This is where Coach Ricky came in. This wonderful man inspired this group of boys to greatness and not just on the field, but in life. He taught them sportsmanship by modeling sportsmanship himself. His approach was one of kindness, whereby he pointed out all the things the individual boys were doing well. He told them how much he enjoyed watching them play—a message he delivered not just once or twice during the season, but every single game. He pushed the good players to play better, and he encouraged the less-skilled players to work hard to get better. He was competitive and driven, but he was also inspirational, and that's what got the boys working as hard as they did. In fact, he nicknamed the team Hard Work, and throughout the season, when we cheered for the boys, we shouted, "Go, Hard Work."

When they messed up, this coach talked to them; but far more often than discussing their mistakes, he pointed out what each boy did well. His spirit, attitude, and energy were never anxious, let alone frenetic. He was poised, relaxed, confident—qualities that rubbed off on his team. I have never seen my son work so hard, practicing off the court and committed to getting better at every opportunity. As a result, we continue to talk about how "hard work" pays off in many situations in life.

The American Academy of Pediatrics asks us to consider what the goal is for an athlete. Bearing in mind that, according to the AAP, only between 0.2-0.5% of high school athletes ever make it to the professional levels of any sport, this is an important question. Why so much emphasis on something that, with the rare exception, isn't going to become a career for our children?

The AAP proposes that "the ultimate goal of youth participation in sports should be to promote lifelong physical activity, recreation, and skills of healthy competition that can be used in all facets of future endeavors." They go on to explain:

Education of parents, athletes, and coaches must be part of the plan to promote fun, skill development, and success for each individual athlete. Skilled young athletes must be mentored carefully to prevent over-participation, which may affect them physically as well as psychologically. Ultimately, it is important for the practitioner to discuss the underlying motivation for sport participation with the athlete, the parent, and, possibly, the coach. Unfortunately, too often the goal is skewed toward adult (parent/coach) goals either implicitly or explicitly. The parent often hopes the child will get a scholarship, become a professional athlete, or fulfill the parents' unfulfilled childhood dreams. It is best to identify and focus on the child's motivation and goals to provide guidance.

Given these clear and concise words from the AAP, what are you doing to inspire greatness in *your* young athlete? If they are learning true greatness, they will become a force for inclusiveness and kindness on their campus. They will be the kind of individual who draws the disenfranchised out of their alienation and makes them feel part of a team. They will accomplish more than all our technology and all our campus security in the battle against school violence.

CHAPTER 18

The Importance of Taking the Rough with the Smooth

HAVE YOU EVER had someone say to you, "I had a dream about you last night"? When someone comes into our awareness in a dream, they usually aren't quite the same as the person we actually know in everyday life assuming they are someone we know at all. But even when they are someone we know, the person themselves has nothing to do with our dream because the dream is entirely of our making. It doesn't actually involve the other person because all of the characters in a dream are of our own making.

If the characters in a dream are something we create, why are they there? In my own life, I have observed how I create them to show me something about *myself*. All the characters in our dreams are a reflection of an aspect of ourselves. They mirror what we can't yet consciously detect in ourselves.

But is this essentially different from everyday life? Are the people in our everyday lives actually known by us for who they *really* are?

To illustrate how we project onto our children, and why

it's important to withdraw our projections and begin to see them in their own right, I'd like to turn to what's ostensibly a children's story, although in truth it's addressed to the child at the heart of each of us, no matter what our age. The story reveals what's entailed in learning to see someone in their own true light.

In 1943, the French aviator Antoine de Saint-Exupery penned one of the most famous children's stories ever written. *The Little Prince* has sold over 140 million copies and continues to sell in huge numbers each year. Currently, it's popularity is being helped by the newly animated movie featuring the little fellow's journeys. I mention this insightful little book because it wonderfully illustrates the point I'm making about not actually knowing others for who they are.

The little prince, who lives on an asteroid, meets a rose who becomes the love of his life. The flower represents meeting "the woman of your dreams" or "the man of your dreams." But even though the prince is head-over-heels in love, he isn't really seeing his flower. He's looking at her as we all look at the people in our life. He's projecting his ideal onto her. He sees her beauty, and he also notices she's quite vain; but he has no real idea who she is yet.

The same can be said of how we project our expectations onto our friends, parents, people at work, and other significant relationships.

People also project onto their doctors, ministers, and therapists. All kinds of expectations are hung on these roles, each of them projections of our idealizations.

What's not obvious at first is that idealizations are a cover story for our neediness. This is why, when people don't live up to the way we have lionized them, we turn around and demonize them. How dare they fail to meet our needs!

In the language of the branch of psychology known as object relations, instead of seeing people in a holistic manner, whereby we integrate both their strong points and their weaknesses into a single idea of them, we tend to objectify them by splitting them into either "all good" (as we lionize) or "all bad" (as we demonize.) Once demonized, we now see them as "the cause of all our problems." We've lost sight of the *person* pretty much altogether. In its extreme form, you see this in how, during the Vietnam war, the North Vietnamese were objectified as "gooks," as if they weren't human.

Idealizing someone, followed by scapegoating them for what's wrong in our life when they fail to match our dreams, or as the enemy in war, is a cover for our own feelings of inadequacy—our sense of neediness. What we don't realize is that the person who doesn't live up to our ideal is doing us a favor. To disillusion us that we can find fulfillment in another person is one of the most important roles any kind of close relationship plays in our life.

When the little prince's euphoria over his rose wore off, he was so disappointed that he even fled his own asteroid for a year. Descending to Earth because his dream lover disappointed him, he experienced a series of situations and encounters that finally began to wake him up to what love is really all about.

It turns out that it's not at all straightforward to wake up and notice another person for who they truly are. The process of becoming acquainted with someone as a real person is one of beginning to see clearly who the other is, free of our projections, which happens *only to the degree we see clearly who we are*. As the little prince underwent this opening of his eyes, he at last became capable of returning to his asteroid to cherish his rose, warts and all. His story mirrors the path all of us need to tread if we are to be capable of loving another, and in no area of life is this more so than with our children.

What the little prince learned centers on kindness. He learned to look not critically at his rose, which caused him to become reactive to her, but in a kind way. It's through the eyes of kindness that we begin to see people as they truly are.

Why We Project onto Others—Especially Our Children

When we project onto another, our mind has a dreamlike filter on it. The way to remove this filter is to self-confront. How are we to do this? How to break out of the dream, or in some cases the nightmare, of the way we see other people, in particular our children?

If we want to shed our projections, instead of asking why a person isn't matching up to our expectations, we should ask *why we have expectations in the first place*. What are these expectations really about? When we ask this question of ourselves, we discover that through our dream of the other we are seeking to supply something we believe to be missing in ourselves.

In other words, our idealizing of others revolves around

a feeling of neediness. We idealize a person because we believe they are going to at last satisfy our deep longing to feel complete, fulfilled, with our life at last meaningful.

The flip side of idealizing, as we've been seeing, is that we demonize and very possibly scapegoat. As one mother of two teenage girls and a boy approaching puberty said, "These kids are a nightmare.

They are the bane of my life. I should never have had kids. Each time, I got pregnant only because my marriage was so boring." This mother may have stated this more starkly than most are willing to do, but the fact she really didn't know why she was having children speaks to so many mothers who give birth not purposefully, with a clear understanding of what it means to bring a child into the world and raise that child, but in an attempt to fulfill some ideal of motherhood and family.

This mother, like so many, was exhilarated by the birth of her children. It was in the aftermath, as the challenges they presented intensified, that she began to resent them, scapegoating them for how chaotic her life had become. Her dream, based on projecting an imaginary ideal, had gone kaput.

When the one we see as our dream lover, dream child, dream supervisor, dream minister, or dream doctor becomes tarnished in our eyes, and we now start demonizing them—and you would be surprised just how many parents do demonize their children, viewing them as if they were a nightmare—the trick to breaking the spell is to ask the same question we need to ask whenever we find ourselves idealizing someone, which is what in *us* this newfound hostility toward the person means. What, in us, flipped the switch whereby the one we adored especially the child we were so thrilled had come into our life now seems like a deranged monster?

At the root of the problem is the fact that we are looking to someone else to complete us, fulfill our dreams, make us happy. This is why we idolize movie stars, pop stars, and sports stars, as well as at times our doctors, clergy, professors, therapists, those in Congress, and other people society casts in the role of pillars of society as if we needed pillars to prop us up. However, these projections are in some ways less immediate and more remote, and therefore less damaging, whereas the projections we load onto our children can be extremely harmful. They have the power to make or break for a child.

All of this emanates from a mistaken sense that we are in some way inadequate.

If you ask pretty much any parent what the gift is a parent can present to a child that will do more to further the child's future than any other— one gift that makes up for a whole heap of inadequacies in any child's upbringing what would their answer be? You are probably thinking that this gift is love. My answer is that it is if we understand what love really is. But sadly, an awful lot of ill treatment, neglect, putting down, and in other ways damaging our children flies under the banner of "love."

Much of what we call love is really quite conditional, in that we give in hope of getting something in return; and when a child isn't forthcoming in the way we require, we often withdraw our affection. Kindness goes out the window and in marches discipline.

Love Is Different from What Many of Us Think It Is

What, really, is love? To understand this is perhaps the most important aspect of this book. It's at the heart of what kindness is all about.

If we look to the world's great spiritual paths for guidance, beneath the many facades many of them have taken on over the centuries is a core truth shared by each of them. This truth has to do with the nature of our being. These paths, each in their different ways, highlight a core insight into our humanity, which is that far from being inadequate, each of us is a manifestation of a fullness, a richness, a diversity of expression that emanates from the heart of the cosmos.

Based on their insight that it isn't an emptiness that's at the core of a human being, but a fullness, these great wisdom traditions emphasize that the attachment so widely mistaken for love and rooted in a feeling of lack, incompleteness, and therefore need is a misunderstanding of our true state.

When we feel empty inside, we imagine the only answer to our yearning is to latch onto someone—a partner, a parent, a child—to fill this void. A child is particularly susceptible to being used in this way because we have so much power to shape children to fit our ideal. But when we look to a child to complete us by fulfilling our dreams, we risk committing a form of child abuse.

To a large extent, we get our sense of who we are from the roles we play in our symbiotic relationships. Trying to fill up our emptiness by getting someone to love us, we imagine such relationships to be our ticket to escaping our insecurity, vulnerability, neediness, and inner loneliness. Consequently, what commonly passes for love is the opposite of love, as we confuse attachment with caring.

When children are used to support our ego, what we offer them as "love" is in reality a needy clinging. The child becomes a means of salving our feelings of inadequacy. Because we need the child to fill up our illusory emptiness, much of the time we simply can't act in the child's best interests. We can't give the most important of all gifts.

The feeling that we are empty, dependent, needy isn't our real state. As we saw in our discussion of desire in an earlier chapter, we are really a fullness seeking to be expressed. Desire is feeling delightful, and wanting to express this wonderful feeling more and more in everyday life. Having a child is a means of experiencing our own ability to delight in life, and we get to bask in the fulfillment that comes from helping another discover and revel in their own joy.

This raises the question, if we are really full and not empty, how did we ever get to feeling so needy? Every child begins life with a good feeling of itself. But in growing up, to varying degrees this good feeling gets buried as parental agendas override the child's need to grow and express itself on its own terms. In place of feeling wonderful, children then begin to experience self-doubt. Instead of a sense of their competence, they start to feel inadequate. As they grow, they may try to cover over their flagging sense of value by polishing a self-image, but the anxiety about themselves sown by the crushing of their natural self seethes beneath the egoic image they project out into the world.

Living out of the emptiness of a lack of an authentic soul fuels neediness. We embark on an endless search for a repetition of that earliest childhood experience of feeling wonderful—a primal sense of ourselves that was originally linked to a mother of whom we were once a part, supported by a father who helped us grasp the concept of someone who is "other." We spend our years seeking to recapture the oceanic bliss we knew in the womb, with our whole life now driven by a search for an identity—a search that dominates our career choices, our relationships, our style of life, and our activities.

The parental task is to help our children discover, hold onto, and develop the fullness of being at their center. This fullness of being is the basis of all love, and its loss in infancy is what drives the controlling, manipulative neediness that so widely passes for love.

To recapitulate, each of us is a far richer, deeper, fuller person than we have ever imagined. To love is to experience the inherent good feeling of ourselves, which we then share with those in whose lives we participate. In other words, quite the opposite of need, inadequacy, feeling incomplete, fear, or anxiety, love is a sense of our own fullness bursting at the seams. To grow in love is to feel our own delightful self in an expanded way, as connection with another draws out more of our fullness. Buoyed on this tide of good feeling, we become kindness personified.

Kindness floods forth from us in how we treat our children, a significant other, our parents, the people we work among and socialize with indeed, everyone with whom our path intersects. It renders a Bernie Madoff an impossibility, a Columbine or Sandy Hook simply unthinkable.

When parents come from their own fullness, each becomes a companion on life's journey instead of a crutch for our ailing sense of self. We quite naturally find ourselves wanting to do those things that, without violating our good feeling of ourselves, bring joy to others. This is the essence of kindness.

CHAPTER 19

Finding Your Own Center of Gravity

AS PARENTS, the best gift we ever give our children is the kindness that flows from being grounded in our own center of gravity. We can assure our children we love them over and over and many do, after having beaten the living daylights out of the kid. But if the love we feel in our hearts doesn't translate into treating our children with a kindness that affirms their personhood, our words are ultimately empty.

In an earlier chapter, I talked extensively about the importance of parents getting a life of their own. In this concluding chapter, I especially want to speak to mothers on this topic, particularly to offer some concrete steps toward creating a life for yourself if you are finding that it's opposed by individuals who are important to you.

When I say I want to speak to moms, it isn't because dads don't also need to understand what I wish to share, but simply because the issue I want to address tends to be more of a problem for mothers, who have long been cast in the traditional role of homemaker even though so many are part of the working world today. Thankfully, things are changing, and indeed have been for some time. Yet for many this change hasn't yet occurred; and even for those of us who have stepped into the new paradigm of equality between the sexes, there's still more that needs to happen. Let me hasten to add that if you are a dad reading this, I hope you'll keep reading, because this is an issue you can help support mom with.

When I speak of being grounded in our own center of gravity, the reason this is so important is that, when we come from this solid place within ourselves, we quite spontaneously sidestep many of the behaviors that get in the way of showing kindness to our children. You see, this center is innately loving. Once we become grounded in it, most of the things that obstruct love in everyday practice melt away.

Because our center is love, it doesn't have to get something in return for the love we show. It doesn't require any kind of validation or reciprocation on the part of our children, which always puts pressure on kids to perform. On the contrary, it's just a wonderful expression of one's own sense of delightfulness and wonderfulness, of which children become the recipients.

Only when a mother is really in touch with her own center of gravity can she love with a love that isn't needy, isn't anxious, isn't clinging, and is therefore freeing of her children's spirit.

A Step by Step Guide to Becoming Your Own Person

Even today, with all the progress made by women as

186

they seek equality, many of us want someone to lean on for a sense of ourselves. Given that women have been schooled for generations to lean on first their father, then their husband, this is no surprise. But women don't need someone to lean on, and the reason men have for thousands of years inoculated women with the belief that they do is to mask their own insecurity. In fact, there's clearly much about women that's stronger than men, so that it's males who are so often needy of someone to prop them up emotionally.

When a woman has been brought up to have her life revolve around a man, it can be difficult for her to locate her center of gravity. For this reason, in case you find yourself struggling with having lost yourself in the tangled web of patriarchy, I want to outline some simple steps for finding your feet.

How this works can be seen in an event in the life of a mother called Priscilla, who was asked to help organize a craft fair. Priscilla's whole life had revolved around her family until now, and Michael, her husband, didn't like the idea of her getting involved in what he saw as an extraneous activity. Nevertheless, Priscilla had a brain that gravitated toward organizing things, and it so happened she had a special appreciation for crafts. She had just never had a chance to use these skills since she embarked on birthing and caring for six children. However, she so wanted to take up the challenge of organizing the craft fair that she managed to talk Michael into begrudgingly agreeing to watch their children on the evenings she would be absent from the home.

Since his wife wasn't present, Michael had to serve

dinner, which taxed his homemaking skills even though Priscilla had prepared everything and left it in the oven. Even as Priscilla was going out the door, assuring him that it would be simple to put the food on the table, he mounted a last stand. "With a rapist on the loose, it's dangerous for a woman to be out alone at night right now," he objected as his wife was preparing to walk out the door at 6:05. When this ploy failed to deter her, he added, "I especially don't like you going out on school nights. What if the children need help with their homework? How can I cope with six children? Your first commitment should be to them."

The meeting was over by nine, and Priscilla's first thought was to rush home to tuck the children into bed. But when she was invited by her girlfriends to stop at a coffee shop on the way home, she cautiously accepted. She knew Michael would be watching the clock, but she reasoned that, with six children, she rarely got out alone and hadn't had coffee with other women in ages.

It was after 10:30 when Priscilla walked in the door. "Where've you been?" Michael growled. "I've been worried about you. I talked to Bob, and Sandy has been home over an hour! Don't you know the children waited up until half-past nine to say goodnight to you? This is what I was afraid would happen, which is why I stressed that your first responsibility is to your family."

Yes, Priscilla does have a responsibility to her family. But were the children harmed by not having their mother available to put them to bed? On the contrary, it's good for children to learn that their mother has a life of her own. Was their father incapable of fixing dinner, helping with homework, reading the children a story, or getting them to bed? Then now was the time to learn.

"You might at least have telephoned," Michael chided, "then I wouldn't have been so worried about you." Of course, it was his own insecurity that was the issue, not Priscilla's safety.

Priscilla could have telephoned, but she might never have enjoyed coffee with her friends, since Michael would have pointed out that she had been out practically the whole evening, informed her that the children were waiting up especially to show her the school project they had completed, and made her feel guilty for even thinking of going for coffee.

At thirty-two years of age, Priscilla is a grown woman who needs neither a chaperone nor a curfew. Neither does she need to answer to Michael, who would do better to confront his insecurity. What Priscilla needs most is to express her own fullness, to live from her own center of gravity, not a center of gravity focused in either her children or her husband.

A mom's best gift is to progressively embrace her own loving soul, in all its blossoming fullness, and thereby awaken the soul of her children that they may blossom in all their magnificence also. Awakened souls are what our world is crying out for.

A Further Bedtime Insight

I talked earlier about bedtimes and how they are a setup intended to help us develop into individuals who can be both true to ourselves and deeply connected, and therefore available to love those we are close to, especially our children.

I also mentioned that my daughter is a sensitive child who is very connected to me. I have worked hard over the past few years to really understand who she is and how I can best interact with her. I mistakenly spent several years rushing her and challenging her, when this was the opposite of what she needs. She craves emotional connection, and quality time spent together is her primary love language.

Each night at bedtime, Faith is the second in the line of bedtime routines, and I lie with her in her bed as we chat and read together. However, on many occasions, by the end of the day I'm tired and end up falling asleep in her bed. I wake up a half hour or so later and go downstairs, but by that time it's almost bedtime for my husband and me. As a result, our quality time together gets cut short many nights. Seeing this, my husband began encouraging me to be more efficient in my bedtime routine with Faith so we can have our adult time. He also knows how much I crave and need my time "off the clock" after the children are asleep.

One evening, I told Faith we would chat and read, then I would lie with her for just a couple of minutes, whereupon I was going to leave her room and go downstairs. This didn't sit well with her at all. But my husband and I need our adult quiet time as well, so I stuck to the plan and was downstairs in record time.

About an hour later, Faith appeared at the top of the stairs and announced that she couldn't sleep. My husband thought this was a thinly veiled attempt to get me up to her room for extra time, so we told her she could read in her bed for a little while until she was ready to fall asleep, and away she went.

When we ourselves went upstairs a little while later, Faith was still awake, claimed she couldn't sleep, and asked me to lie down with her, which I did. My husband thought I was making a mistake. However, within five minutes she was asleep, and I crept out of her room and into our own.

A few minutes later, we heard her door open and she walked into our room. We wondered whether she was then going to want to crawl up into our bed, but she simply said she needed a drink and disappeared into the bathroom. When she came back out, she came to me, looked deeply into my eyes with a warm, satisfied and loving smile, and gave me a hug. Then she went around to the other side of the bed and gave her daddy a hug. Saying goodnight, she told us she loved us and returned to her room.

It all seemed very simple, but my husband suspected this wasn't the last time we would see her that night. I disagreed. I told him that when I looked in her eyes, I intuited that her bucket was full, and that we wouldn't see her again until morning. So we made a friendly little wager, betting a dollar. Guess who won the bet? That's right, she slept through the rest of the night.

A few days later, we had a rerun of this bedtime episode. I'm passionate about my work, and my schedule dictated that I work late two nights in a row, missing my children's bedtime both nights. The kids don't like this when it happens and neither do I, but sometimes it's unavoidable in order for me to pursue my profession, which is such an important aspect of my life.

When I arrived home this particular evening, Faith was

already in bed but not yet asleep, so I went into her room and she was elated to see me. I lay down with her for a few minutes and we had a quick chat about our day. I shared with her some stories about my work, since she understands how much I love helping parents connect more deeply with their children.

While my husband and I were getting ready for bed, Faith came into our room and said she couldn't sleep. I asked her if she would like to crawl up in our bed and snuggle with me. Of course, she agreed. My husband, who was about to take a bath, rolled his eyes at me. "I guarantee she'll be asleep before you're out of the tub," I whispered. Only a couple of minutes later, as Faith lay beside me and I read my book, she fell fast asleep, and my husband carried her back into her bed, where she remained until morning.

When Faith was younger, her strong need for physical closeness used to stress me out, especially when I wanted to be "off the clock" after the children's bedtime. While they are little, it's tough to carve out grownup time. But just as Priscilla had to insist on spending time in an activity she enjoyed, as well as talking with her girlfriends, I've had to evolve as a parent and make sure I balance my needs with those of my daughter. I understand the need for her bucket to be filled, and I make myself available to her when I can. She knows I do my best for her, which means there's no manipulation on her part, no stalling to try to extract more time from me. When her bucket is full, it's full, and she goes on with her own life, while simultaneously cheering me on as I pursue a career that's so meaningful to me.

Sometime later, over breakfast, Faith told me that in

one of her classes she had needed to write a persuasive essay on why a certain person was important to her. When she told me that she chose me, I smiled, looked into her eyes, gave her a kiss, and asked her what she wrote in her essay. She said she made two main points. First, that I love her and take good care of her; and second, that I understand her very well. Isn't this what parenting is all about? Those two items are the main ingredients of a healthy connection with our children.

Love isn't enough, even when it's deep and strong and powerful. Love with understanding of not only our children, but also ourselves is the magic formula. If we have a mix of these two ingredients, our children know it and feel it.

When the way we relate is based on our strength as moms, fueled by our innate sense of fullness as a person, instead of based in a fallacious belief in our inherent weakness, family interactions become an arena for the expression of more and more of our loving being. They call forth our inherent caring, consideration, and kindness—all of it expressed with graciousness.

How different love is from what we usually call love. What a difference it makes to parenting. As each member of the family grows—the adults and children alike—we become increasingly individuated, and simultaneously more profoundly connected.

No longer trying to be clones, we can at last be close, true companions on the journey, each at our different stage.

Author Erin Taylor and her family.

ABOUT THE AUTHOR

ERIN TAYLOR, MA has worked for almost two decades with families of all kinds, from foster and adoptive families to biological, divorced, blended and single-parent families. She earned her Bachelor's Degree in Psychology from Drexel University and her Master's Degree from Loyola University Maryland.

Erin met her future husband, Jay, when they were 18 and they are now both pursuing careers that they love while joyfully raising their three heart-healthy children. Their first daughter, Sydney who was conceived via In-Vitro Fertilization, died of a heart defect when she was only 24 days old. Erin and Jay founded and for 12 years ran a non-profit organization, the Sydney Mae Taylor Foundation, to help other young people living with heart defects, while maintaining her career as a therapist.

Getting to that balanced, peaceful place as a parent can be a very difficult thing to do. Erin found herself questioning her judgment and decisions, turning to books to help her find her way on the parenting journey. The most profoundly transformational book she discovered was *The Conscious Parent* by Dr. Shefali Tsabary which inspired Erin to dive deeply into Dr. Shefali's teachings.

As a conscious parent teacher, student and parent herself, Erin understands that parents have all the wisdom inside of them that they need to be the exact parents their children need them to be, but in order to access that wisdom, they need to "grow themselves up."

Erin is thrilled to help parents find their way on their parenting journey, helping them to become the parents they always wished to become and have the relationships with their children they only thought was possible in their dreams.

Erin is now a PCI Certified Parent Coach$^©$ helping parents to develop deeper, more fulfilling relationships with their children. Erin believes that parenting is one of the most challenging and sacred tasks we can ever take on in life, while also being the most rewarding and satisfying. She writes a blog and is a regular contributor to South Jersey MOM Magazine and Natural Awakenings South Jersey Edition.

HIRE ERIN

Erin presents workshops and webinars to individuals, groups, and schools
- Introduction to Conscious Parenting
- Raising a Motivated Child
- Transcending Your Triggers
- or customize to your needs

Erin is available for Keynote Speeches, Presentations for large and small audiences.
- Seeing Challenges as Opportunities to Grow
- Gratitude
- or customize to your needs

CONNECT WITH ERIN

http://www.villageparentcoaching.com
Erin's blog: http://www.villageparentcoaching.com/blog/
http://www.facebook.com/ittakesavillageparentcoaching
http://www.twitter.com/parentcoacherin